In our frenetic, stress-filled, work-drunk culture, Jen Wise offers a hope-filled way forward. Rest. Space. Health. Stillness. Quiet. These are ingredients in the recipe for true life in Christ.

Jen's charming stories and warm writing style make this book easy to engage with, but her direct challenge to live a counter-cultural life by embracing the unforced rhythms of grace reminds us it will be costly. But as Jen also reminds us: it's worth it.

—J. R. BRIGGS, AUTHOR OF *FAIL: FINDING HOPE AND GRACE IN THE MIDST OF MINISTRY FAILURE*; FOUNDER, KAIROS PARTNERSHIPS

This book is for anyone who needs to take a step back, regroup, and find God in the messiness of life. Jen as a narrator is both refreshing and honest, leading us into a full conversation about grace, health, and a vibrant life. Take forty days to read this book and watch your attitude and energy change.

—HANNAH BRENCHER, AUTHOR; FOUNDER, MORE LOVE LETTERS; ONLINE EDUCATOR

The
BRIGHT
LIFE

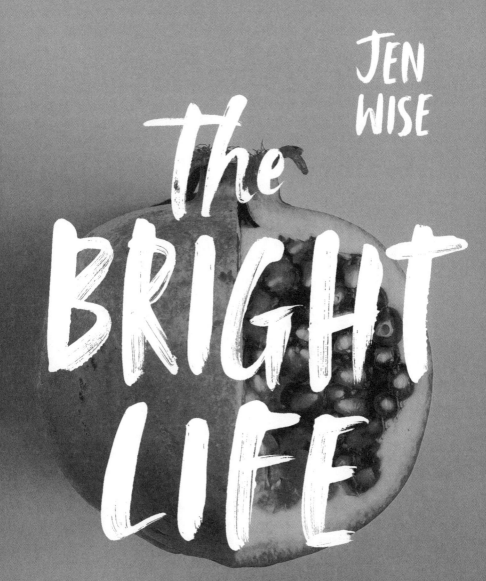

JEN
WISE

The
BRIGHT
LIFE

40 Invitations to Reclaim Your
Energy for the Full Life

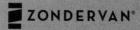

ZONDERVAN®

ZONDERVAN

The Bright Life
Copyright © 2018 by Jen Wise

Requests for information should be addressed to:
Zondervan, *3900 Sparks Dr. SE, Grand Rapids, Michigan 49546*

ISBN 978-0-310-35111-5 (softcover)
ISBN 978-0-310-35113-9 (audio)
ISBN 978-0-310-35112-2 (ebook)

Interior design: Denise Froehlich
Interior illustrations: iStock Photo/mashuk
Cover design: Micah Kandros
Cover photo: zamurovic photography

First printing October 2018 / Printed in the United States of America

For Ellington & Breckin
May you always shine bright

Contents

Introduction

This one goes out to the women whose work is never finished. To the women who are tired—running too hard. To the ones who feel that what they have to give is never enough, that they are not enough. I'm with you.

We can so clearly see the life we want. We get glimpses of how things could be, but there's this relentless, discouraging gap between how things are, and how we want them to be—how we know they should be. We see it in our homes, our families, our world, and maybe, most alarmingly, in ourselves.

So we chase it. We try harder. We cram more into our day—waking early, staying up late. If only we could be a bit more efficient, make no mistakes, then we'd be able to get our homes in order, our careers in order, our families in order, our world in order.

But there are just so many problems. It's overwhelming and heartbreaking. Countries rage, communities rage, families rage—but we know we can help. We're healers. We're not afraid of hard work. We're brave and full of big love. Yet the problems are just as big. And no matter how much we love, and how hard we work, we never see the healed and whole world we long for—but we try, we give, we pour ourselves out.

And we don't skip a beat—there's no grace for ourselves—because if we falter, slow down, take a break, everything will fall to pieces. We'll fail. We'll lose our spot in our social circles. We'll be left behind in our careers. Our children won't thrive. The world will burn. And we'll never achieve that life we want.

Is it any wonder we're crumbling under the pressure? That our minds, bodies, and relationships are running on fumes? We just can't go on this way. I know this is true because I've seen it all come crashing down.

A few years ago, my husband, Jon, began experiencing a growing, inexplicable pain that moved through his limbs. With no answers, his symptoms continued to worsen over a period of eighteen months until one night in January the pain levels skyrocketed. He could barely move, barely get out of bed. I helped him dress to get to the hospital where the doctors told us it was a flare up—of what, they weren't sure. "It will be a long week waiting this out," they said, "but it's just a week."

Jon didn't get any better that week. Instead, he stayed at such a high level of pain for the large majority of that year that he essentially limped out of bed in the morning, worked, hobbled back into the house, and rested until bedtime. On top of this, he experienced a constant parade of side effects and complications associated with the many trial-and-error medications. We had no end in sight, no progress, no proper diagnosis. We were utterly terrified.

Toward the end of that year, we finally got an appointment with a top-level specialist. He took Jon off all of the medications (pills, shots, weekly infusions—the works), and

gave him these instructions: get full nights of sleep, go to yoga and swim, take long weekends away, go to counseling, quit one of your jobs, take up a hobby, and reduce stress. This was the actual prescription. Unreal.

Here's the thing: I had been talking about, writing about, and caring about holistic faith for years. I believed whole-heartedly that our faith in Jesus infiltrates all parts of our lives, not just the traditionally religious elements. Somehow though, it really only manifested in our lives in ways that kept us insanely busy, giving too much of ourselves, and running on empty. We were hospitable to a fault, trying to "make a difference" like we were the only hope of the world, lacking boundaries of any sort, and sleeping only four or five hours a night in order to fit everything in.

We took the doctor's advice and within a couple weeks we saw improvement for the very first time. Groundbreaking.

Since then, it's been a slow and steady climb to health with some bumps and missteps along the way. Somehow, for Jon and I as for many of us, taking care of ourselves is not as second nature as it should be. We tend to gravitate toward overwork, toward trying to get ahead, toward earning approval. The natural way of life is surprisingly unnatural.

We know there's something better. We know what God intended is good and beautiful and the way things are meant to be, but it all feels just out of reach. Because we're tired. We're overwhelmed. And in a lot of ways, we've grown accustomed to settling for the ordinary slogging-through way of life.

But I don't want to slog through. And I don't think you want to, either.

Jesus invites us to a better way, a brighter way. He says, "Are you tired? Worn out? Burned out on religion? Come to me. Get away with me and you'll recover your life. I'll show you how to take a real rest. Walk with me and work with me—watch how I do it. Learn the unforced rhythms of grace" (Matthew 11:28–30 MSG).

Let's walk together for forty days and learn the unforced rhythms of grace. We can live like we know we're loved, accepted, and valued. We can emerge renewed, our lungs filled with fresh air. And we can discover that the bright life we want is ours, if we'll just let go, trust, stop trying so hard. I'm on this journey too—let's go, arm in arm.

Day 1

Coming Undone

In high school, my friends and I thought it would be funny to unscrew desk tops. We'd remove three of the screws underneath, leaving the fourth engaged just enough to hold the top in place. All it took was a little pressure—a bored head leaning on an arm, a shifting in the seat, a stack of crusty text books—and POP! The desk top would fly.

At the time, it was an utterly delightful distraction from the monotony of the school year grind. Looking back, I cannot believe that I participated in this activity or, more honestly, was its founder. But for some reason, neither the destruction-of-property angle, nor the likely-underpaid-custodian-who-had-to-fix-the-desks angle sunk in until adulthood. There was just something so amusing in seeing the slightest bit of pressure send everything into chaos.

This dynamic lost its magic later in life.

In the midst of young children, a young career, and the youthful folly of trying to save the world all by ourselves, Jon and I had come undone. We were always going, always doing, never resting.

We'd fill our days to the brim in the name of not wasting potential. We'd invite people over on any free evenings because hospitality matters, right? We'd stay up until two or three in the morning, furiously typing on our laptops while *30 Rock* reruns looped in the background. Then we'd be up and moving early to get a jump start on the day. We became experts in powering through. Who could sleep anyway when there was so much to do, so many needs in the world, so many projects to join?

Run, run, run. Stay up late. Repeat, repeat, repeat.

Chaos was our default.

We went on like this for years. It was okay though, because we wanted it that way—or that's what we told ourselves. We were high-energy people. We were the ones who could get things done. We would keep going when others would give up (or more likely, go to bed). We weren't going to let our lives just slide by with nothing to show.

What we didn't realize was that while our frantic pace did accomplish some things, it left out quite a few of the most important. Like being refilled. Like allowing time to process and heal. Like quiet, stillness, space, health, and rest.

In the whir of activity, everything came loose and the one screw left was just barely hanging on. All it took was one rude email from a coworker, one ill-timed computer glitch, one child refusing to use a sane amount of toothpaste, and that top was flying off.

What would, in another lifetime, be a normal everyday stressor, a hiccup in the day, sent me flailing. Why is everyone so mean? Why is Apple trying to destroy me? When will my life play out the way I think it should?

I can throw a good tantrum.

But it was more than a tantrum. Because while there might be an immediate outburst of frustration, more so there was despair—that nothing would ever be fully right, in our lives or in our world, no matter how hard we tried. There was loneliness in wondering if relationships even mattered when it seemed that everyone was looking to get something out of us. And there was a mounting fear that came with knowing that we were hanging on by a thread. *How much more can I take?*

And yet we didn't slow down. Slowing down was not an option, it was defeat. Slowing down was giving in, giving up. I could visualize the life we were after, the world we dreamt of, and the only way to get there was to work harder, to go above and beyond with difficult people, to put in more effort, to give and try and give some more.

We all experience this. We can picture the way our families should be, the way our careers should be, the way our houses should be, and the way we, ourselves, should be. But no matter how hard we try it's just out of reach. Our careers aren't as meaningful as we had hoped, someone spilled dog food all over the kitchen floor, and we don't even have time to do our hair let alone eat a healthy breakfast.

As Christians, this affects us on a much larger scale as well. It's not just our home décor or nine-to-five that are lacking. We see it in the world around us. We know that God created this world to be beautiful and vibrant. He created us to care for one another and this earth, and to cultivate peace. He created us to live in loving communion with himself. But, most of the time, our reality isn't like that.

Reality is struggle, poverty, violence, exhaustion. Reality is conflict, stress, disparity, loneliness, pollution, and hate.

Wars rage abroad, in our communities, and in our own hearts.

We are keenly aware of the gap between how things are, and how things should be—in our lives and in our world. If only we could just try harder, do better, invest more. Maybe we could finally have that happy family in the happy community on top of the world with a giant smiley face painted on its side. (Also, I'd like everyone to be holding hands in one giant ring around the earth, swaying to "I'd Like to Teach the World to Sing.")

With all this trying and working and giving and investing, you'd think we'd be further along. But here's the thing: When we give everything we've got, we have nothing left. We're empty. We have no room for errors, for stressors, for rude coworkers, for children who won't listen, for the stranger who looks at us the wrong way, or the friend who is just as run-down and empty as we are and lets it show.

How will our world or our lives ever resemble the peace and beauty we aspire to when we're all depleted and have no room left for grace?

As Jon and I whirred on in our default chaos, I began to wonder if maybe we were going about this all wrong. Maybe the life we want is a gift freely given, and we're over here twisting and pulling and tearing at the packaging—cracking it to pieces in an attempt to get into it—while all the while a simple set of instructions says, "Gently pull here."

Could it really be that easy? Paul tells us in Romans that it is. In chapter five he writes, "We throw open our doors to God and discover at the same moment that he has already thrown open his door to us. We find ourselves standing where

we always hoped we might stand—out in the wide open spaces of God's grace and glory, standing tall and shouting our praise" (Romans 5:2 MSG).

Is it possible the life God wants for us is right there waiting if we'd just stop trying so hard? Are beauty and peace and wide open spaces available to each one of us if we simply slow down, and gently receive the gift we've been given?

LOOKING INWARD: Consider the ways that your real life, the real world, and the real you don't match up to your ideals. How do you feel when you bump up against this disparity? Do you ever overextend yourself trying to close this gap?

LOOKING UPWARD: Confess to God the ways in which you stress and strive to fix yourself and your world. Thank him for making a way for us to be made new and whole through his Son, Jesus. Praise him for being faithful to his promise to set all things right, to heal what's broken.

LOOKING OUTWARD: Prayerfully choose one area where you regularly find yourself doing too much, giving too much, in an effort toward perfection—the perfect house, the perfect children, the perfect church. When you feel the frantic pull to work harder, to try harder in this way, choose one tangible task to let go. Lay it down and step into the wide open spaces of God's grace.

Day 2

Crying in Yoga

I can still remember the first time it happened—lying on the floor surrounded by strangers, in complete silence, tears streaming from my eyes. No matter my level of embarrassment, I could not make it stop.

Let's back up.

I fell in love with yoga several years ago. I think it happened when I finally made that invisible but important shift from "wanting to be skinny" to "wanting to be healthy." Somehow I had made it into adulthood without giving a thought to my body other than how it looked in a pair of jeans. My first brush with yoga was like flipping on a gigantic switch. I was suddenly aware of how posture affects overall health, how muscle tone impacts internal organs, and that flexibility is grossly underrated. (People of the world, you should be able to touch your toes!) I quickly became a faithful attendee at my local studio.

For you non-yogis, each session runs through a series of poses—some simple, many quite challenging. There's a lot of mental work too. Balance on one foot, exhale at these times,

keep shoulders back and down, hold arms at this angle, flex muscles in this order. It takes quite a bit of focus. However, once we put the work in we're rewarded with *savasana*, the final resting pose. After a period of physical and mental intensity, we lay flat on our backs, our bodies at ease, in recovery.

This is when the crying started.

I was stunned. And embarrassed. And very, very confused. Here I was, minding my own business, squeezing in a workout in the middle of a full day, and suddenly I'm using my ponytail as a tissue. What was I even crying about?

I walked home in a daze. I guess it was fair to say I was under some stress. Yes, Jon and I were busy as usual, but Jon had been having some health problems as well. And after months of mounting pain and no proper diagnosis, his doctor had begun to work through a series of medications, hoping one would take.

This seemingly trial-and-error approach wasn't great. Every next-level medication arrived with its own next-level side effects. Strange rashes would cover entire swaths of Jon's back. He'd text me from the restroom at work saying he would be home late because he couldn't stop vomiting long enough to even make it to the parking garage.

But we were toughing it out. It seemed best to just work a little harder to keep things rolling. What were we supposed to do? Let everything we held fall apart? Not to mention that Jon has never been one to just chill. It took five years of marriage before I could convince him to throw on a pair of sweats in the evening. Even on the rare occasion that we turned on a movie, he would sit there in work clothes, shoes on, as if a meeting could break out at any moment. At least I knew how to properly veg (albeit with a computer in my lap).

So we carried on our normal frenetic pace with the fun twist of squeezing in doctor's visits, blood draws, and a host of prescription-induced abnormalities.

But as it turns out, for most of us, when we're overloaded all day with tangible needs we tend to stuff the nontangible needs aside. And when we're attending to all the to-dos, we neglect tending our own souls. And when we do this for too long, it may only take a few minutes of still, calm, silence for all those buried feelings and emotions to surface. Who knew?

When we run too fast, it's easy to not feel. It's easy to deny our wounds, fears, and insecurities. But contrary to what we might tell ourselves, we're not brushing them off and we're not letting them go. We're stuffing them deep down inside because we don't have the bandwidth to sort through these kinds of complicated emotions.

That's what I had done. Sure, I had to take on more as Jon's abilities weakened. And yes, medical issues add a strain to your schedule. But busyness wasn't just a necessity to manage my growing responsibilities. Busyness was a comfort—it was a shield. Because exhaustion was better than having to feel the pain and the fear I wanted to ignore.

No, I don't need help with anything. It's much easier to run myself into the ground than to acknowledge that I'm broken. I'd much prefer to assemble this patio furniture myself on a blazing-hot summer day than be gifted with an afternoon to slow down and recognize how terrified I am.

Sometimes our true feelings are really uncomfortable. Of course we try to bury them. But they're still there under the surface, feeding into all areas of our life—our relationships,

our reactions, our bodies. And the longer we ignore them, the more they grow and the greater unchecked influence they hold.

Three minutes of rest on my yoga mat had been just enough of a pause for my fear and sadness to break through. I couldn't pretend that I was unfazed by Jon's sickness. I couldn't lie to myself and say that I wasn't worried.

I had to admit that our life was not what I had pictured for us. I had to admit that I was terrified that my future was insecure and unknown—that I might soon have a husband who could no longer go for walks, play in the yard with the kids, or even stand around making small talk at school events—that the financial stability of our family might soon rest solely on my shoulders. I had to admit that I was angry—at God, at the unfairness of all of this, and at myself for not being as strong as I needed to be.

It felt terrible. I didn't want these to be my feelings. I didn't want this to be my life. But here's the thing: Those were my real feelings, and this was my real life. All I needed was a little space to recognize it.

We could all use a little more space. We need space to let our breathing slow to a normal rhythm, to hear the thoughts rolling around in the corners of our mind, to feel our real feelings, real hurts. We need space to understand the aches and hopes that dwell down deep, muffled but not silenced.

What if we were willing to slow down and listen to our hearts? What if we weren't afraid to let our true feelings, hopes, and fears out into the light? Maybe we can only make progress in our journey once we're willing to stand boldly at the starting line. Will you join me there?

LOOKING INWARD: Is there a part of you that feels more comfortable keeping yourself busy and occupied? Why? What feelings could you be burying under that mound of activities and to-dos?

LOOKING UPWARD: Ask God to shine light into the darker corners of your heart—invite him to bring to the forefront relationships, pain, worries, and struggles that you've been sidelining. Praise him for his kindness to walk with us even in these places we'd rather avoid.

LOOKING OUTWARD: Where can you open up some space to listen to your real feelings, hopes, and fears? It's okay to start small. Consider switching your phone to sleep mode after dinnertime. Choose a day per week for a social media fast. Start each day alone with a cup of coffee and a journal—or simply in silence.

Day 3

Feeding Worry

I open the door to every public restroom like there might be a dead body inside. Because there might be! I'm not even joking. I swing that door open wide and let my eyes sweep the room before entering. It may be unlikely to stumble upon a heinous crime scene in my local Starbucks, but that doesn't make it impossible. And once a thought like this has entered my mind, it makes itself at home.

This is why I don't watch scary movies or scary television shows. I find it impossible to un-see the horrific images—I can't un-know the terrifying possibilities that apparently exist all around me. I have a predisposition toward worry and fear. I don't need to feed that tendency.

Sometimes, though, we can't avoid bumping up against this stuff. We can't always just click away. We'd have to live in a bubble to avoid hearing about terror attacks, violent crimes, natural disasters, and newly spreading diseases. Not to mention, we encounter plenty of reasons to feel unnerved in our own daily lives.

For me, as Jon's health grew worse, my fear grew with it. I worried incessantly. I worried about how we'd get through the next day. I worried how we'd survive the year. I worried what it would look like to grow old together—what my future would look like if Jon wasn't able to walk, use his hands, or even get out of bed.

I worried about our kids. How many activities had Jon missed? How many experiences had he sat out on because he wasn't physically able to participate? How was this affecting them? What level of worry, sadness, frustration, and hurt were they feeling? Would I ever come close to filling the gap?

I worried about Jon. How long can someone live in this amount of pain? How did he feel missing so much of life— watching friends carry on with delightfully ordinary activities, sitting to the side while his kids tossed the football in the street, seeing me run around the house taking care of tasks that used to be his? Was I any comfort, or did he feel utterly alone?

Nighttime was the worst. By the time we went to bed, we were both spent, physically and emotionally. Jon would fall instantly asleep, but the pain kept him from sleeping soundly, and he'd toss and turn and groan in pain throughout the night. Meanwhile, I'd lay next to him, feeling his movement, hearing his body beg for relief, with tears streaming down my face.

One night I moved to the couch, desperate to escape the constant reminder of how bleak all of this was. But I still laid awake, mind racing. It felt wrong to abandon Jon in our room alone. I felt like a traitor being able to take a break from what he couldn't escape. We would sleep, or not sleep, in our bed together.

So each day we pushed through—or maybe limped through—our tasks and to-dos. And each night, with the distractions out of the way, we laid next to each other in a jumble of pain, fear, worry, and sadness.

I wished I could pray. I wished I wanted to pray. But I felt empty at best, and angry the rest of the time. My middle-of-the-night worries had nowhere to go, no way to be soothed. Why ask God for help, comfort, or peace, when he had seemingly abandoned us? I wouldn't even know how to pray with sincerity, because in all my begging for healing, petitioning for health, Jon had only gotten progressively worse. I didn't know what to say to a God that I believed in, but didn't particularly like anymore.

Yet there was still a spark of hope, buried inside, that wanted to believe in God's goodness, trust he was still here, in all of this, somehow. It had been a while since I had cared much for reading Scripture—it just felt like a reminder of something I used to naively believe but now had been rudely awakened to the realities of the world. Which is why it could only be the grace of God that I stumbled upon this passage in the book of Romans.

In chapter eight, Paul writes this, "Meanwhile, the moment we get tired in the waiting, God's Spirit is right alongside helping us along. If we don't know how or what to pray, it doesn't matter. He does our praying in and for us, making prayer out of our wordless sighs, our aching groans. He knows us far better than we know ourselves, knows our pregnant condition, and keeps us present before God. That's why we can be so sure that every detail in our lives of love for God is worked into something good" (Romans 8:26–28 MSG).

Relief.

Maybe I didn't know how or what to pray, but I knew wordless sighs, and I sure knew aching groans. My heart was struggling to draw near to God—but according to this passage, I could rest, knowing that God's Spirit would pray in me, for me, and keep me present before God. And sometimes, isn't that all we can do? Allow God's Spirit to do what we wish we could?

Sometimes we allow our fear to get the best of us. Our circumstances feel crushing, and our worries overwhelming. We become riddled with anxiety. We feel panicked and abandoned—our prayers seem like they're vanishing into thin air. We don't see the resolution we're looking for.

So we grasp for control. We just need more systems, more organization, more energy, then we'll be able to sort out these problems for ourselves. With a little more hard work we should finally find relief, security. But it never works that way, does it?

In fact, Paul is telling us that God is at work, his Spirit is right alongside us. We don't need to go into overdrive—we simply need to rest as his Spirit petitions for us, works for us, and turns our pain and tears into prayers. Isn't that beautiful? And this passage says that this is "why we can be so sure that every detail in our lives of love for God is worked into something good" (v. 28).

I want to be so sure. Is it possible that we can drop the worry, concede control, and find the rest we need? Is it possible that if we patiently wait, God will take all of these broken pieces of our lives and our hearts and craft something good? As we wait and see, let's find comfort in knowing that

while we are so weak, God's spirit is unwavering, holding us up to the One who is strong.

LOOKING INWARD: What worries dominate your mind? What answers, actions, changes have you been expectantly praying for and awaiting?

LOOKING UPWARD: Thank the Lord for giving us comfort, peace, and an advocate through his Spirit (John 14:26–27). Sit quietly and trust that through the Spirit you are present before God.

LOOKING OUTWARD: When you feel yourself sighing—exhausted, stressed, worn down—remember that the Spirit knows you, knows your heart, and is praying in you and for you. Rather than donning your cape in an attempt to save the day, allow his presence to bring you comfort and peace.

Day 4
Light Streaks Through

"I hope this is okay—but I asked around and got a recommendation for a doctor for Jon. He's top in his field in the country. I'll send the info." It was my first text from Sharna. We had about a million mutual friends and were just starting to get to know each other better. Several of us had started to meet here and there for a Bible study, and a core group kind of just clicked.

I hadn't been a part of a group like this in years, and after our very first week, I realized how much I had missed it. There is just something special about a safe place to open up, friends who encourage you to better things, and also a little weekly kick in the butt to get into Scripture. I needed all three of these things.

Jon and I had been wading through this season, somewhat secretly, for over a year, when I opened up to this group about his health—and Sharna, being Sharna, immediately jumped into action to make connections and help out. I was so grateful.

I passed her text on to Jon, "Call right away."

He did. It was May. And the next available appointment was mid-August.

So we waited. It was our only option—and if we'd made it this long, we could make it another few months.

Summer arrived and we headed to Traverse City, Michigan—a special beach town oasis where we hide away for most of the summer. I was a jumble of emotions. Summers in Traverse City are one of the highlights of my year. I always look forward to extended time with family, lazy days at the beach, and working my way through the unique cafés and restaurants downtown. This year was extra special because my little sister was marrying her perfect match. Normally, our summer away is a nice breather from ordinary life, but this year, our ordinary life wasn't so ordinary, and there was no way to leave it behind.

On our way to TC we stopped in Grand Rapids for dinner with good friends. Sitting outside in the cutest, happiest taqueria, laughing and clinking glasses with kindred spirits, we could—for the moment—pretend everything was fine, pretend we were fine. And it felt so good.

But it didn't last. As soon as we hopped in the car into continue north, reality quickly returned, bringing a host of new complications. Jon's feet and legs were swelling like balloons. A quick call to the doctor left us with more questions. Was the swelling a new symptom of the unknown condition? Was it a side effect of one of his prescriptions? Or was it heart failure—a possibility based on his combination of medications?

When we pulled into town, Jon dropped me at the little apartment we'd rented and went straight to the hospital. He came home the next morning with the complications cleared,

but no new answers. We tried to make the most of our time, but every day was like riding the rough waves of Lake Michigan—ups and downs, free floating for just a moment, and then bowled over.

This all seemed so wrong. We had worked so hard, given everything we had. And while our life wasn't perfect, we had found some level of success, some level of what we'd wanted. Sure, we didn't necessarily want to run so hard forever, but isn't that what it takes to make it, to land on your feet? So we had put in the time, the effort, and it worked. But just when we thought we had our footing, we'd been swiped out at the legs. It all felt so unfair.

Mid-August came, and we packed up our beach towels, sunscreen, and tennis racquets and headed back to the East Coast. Jon's appointment was a few days away and I wanted to be hopeful, but felt nervous. All he'd received from doctors so far was a personal pharmacy and terrifying side effects. When there was no improvement from one appointment to the next, the answer was always higher doses, added prescriptions. We'd question the advice, the drugs, but with no other direction, we were at a loss.

When the day of the appointment came, the doctor took in Jon's medical history. After a year and a half of worsening symptoms, trial-and-error medical treatments, and no answers, we finally got a proper diagnosis. To put it simply, Jon's body was reacting to years of too much stress and too little rest—too much breaking, too much pouring out, and not nearly enough of being put back together.

Years of stress, with no space for rest and recovery, had all his wires crossed. His central nervous system was going haywire, and it would take time and intentional change for his body to begin to untangle itself.

Some people are prescribed pills and liquids and shots. Our prescription? Sleep. And yoga. And recreation. And long weekends. And less work, less stress. The doctor pulled Jon off all the meds, which at this point consisted of a handful of pills plus weekly infusions. I've never been so happy to say goodbye to something.

For the first time in a long time, we felt hope. Standing at the bottom of this mountain was daunting—we knew there was so much work to do, that this was a long journey, that we may never reach the peak—but at least we were on the right path.

The next morning, I watched Jon hobble out of bed and put together a gym bag, every laborious movement a window into his pain. His doctor had suggested he start with swimming. It would be painful, but it was gentle on the body. So off he went. It was excruciating. But he went. Every morning, and often again after work. And for a short time after the swim, he'd feel better than he had in a while.

Stroke after stroke, lap after lap, day after day, the slowest and slightest and most painful improvement—but it was there. Incredibly, it doesn't matter how dark it's been, hope is found in the sliver of light that peeks through.

Isn't that always the way with God? When we're living in our own mess, lost and exhausted, we see that he's cracked open a door. Light streaks through; he's provided a way. We begin to hold a little more tightly to the promise that one day this world will be made right—we will be made right.

First Peter 1:3–5 (MSG) invites us into the light, into the hope we've found, the promise he's made to see us through.

"What a God we have! And how fortunate we are to have him, this Father of our Master Jesus! Because Jesus was raised from the dead, we've been given a brand-new life and have everything to live for, including a future in heaven—and the future starts now! God is keeping careful watch over us and the future. The Day is coming when you'll have it all—life healed and whole."

A life healed and whole. We want that with everything in us, right? Friends, it's coming. It may be a slow climb, but this future, this brand-new life, it's a promise, and it starts now.

Can you see it? Can you find the light peeking through? Even when everything seems wrong, broken. Even when we feel tired, worn down. God's promise to heal us and set things right still stands and he graces us with reminders of this truth if we have eyes to see it. Let's drop the worry and look for the streams of light, for God's bright reminder of his promises to us.

LOOKING INWARD: Are you able to see light peeking through the darkness? Can you hold on to God's promises, even when life is tough, the climb is slow? What encourages you? What makes it difficult to have faith?

LOOKING UPWARD: God has given us brand-new life, and the promise of completing his work in us and our world—of a life healed and whole. Thank him for this. Meditate on it. Rest in it.

LOOKING OUTWARD: The future starts now. What can you do today to live into the healed and whole life we're promised? What small step is God calling you to take?

Day 5

What's Your Slap Bracelet?

A couple years ago, Jon and I scrambled around town, hitting stores we normally avoid, putting together a couple of very interesting ensembles. Our dear friends Lauren and Jesse were throwing a '90s party, and we knew the costumes would be outstanding. These people are the ultimate hosts, and when they throw a party or gather a few friends, everyone knows it's going to be a night to remember.

We had brainstormed for weeks, coming up blank. With the party just a day away, I was wondering if we'd be forced to just show up in a bunch of spandex. Fortunately, I remembered my secret weapon—my friend Christie, who is my go-to for all kinds of inquiries. Whereas I had struggled for weeks to come up with some direction, Christie knew immediately. "Justin Timberlake and Britney Spears, of course. From the '90s, when they were dating."

She was right. Jon was tall with curly hair. I had a friend with access to a girls' school uniform. With minimal shopping, a little hair gel (for him), and a little braiding (for me), we'd be on our way.

We arrived at the party in our ridiculous outfits and fit right in. Britney and Justin joined the company of Wayne and Garth, Madonna and Michael Jackson, Cher from *Clueless*, and a slew of other notable '90s celebs. We were immediately engulfed in '90s bliss. The music, the games, the prizes. They even had a pogo ball. (Did you forget about pogo balls?) It was pure joy.

The '90s were full of all sorts of outlandishness that many of us loved with our whole hearts. Pogo balls are definitely toward the top of that list. Also, decorating everything with puffy paint. And crimping our hair. And all things neon. And let's not forget the queen of all '90s accessories: the slap bracelet.

Slap bracelets were a phenomenon. Everyone who was anyone had a slap bracelet. I distinctly remember sitting in class, looking around at the cool patterns and fun colors on my friends' wrists. At recess and lunch all the girls would repeatedly slap their bracelets on. Slap, remove, straighten, repeat.

I didn't want anything more than I wanted a slap bracelet. They were so cool. It would make me so cool. It would make me confident. It would change my life. I'd be so happy I'd never want anything again.

One weekend, my parents drove me to the mall and bought a slap bracelet for me from Claire's. This was the moment I'd been waiting for. I slapped it on and waited to feel incredible, awesome, like a teenager.

It didn't happen.

I wore it to school on Monday, sure it would impress, sure I'd have a bit more swagger. At recess and lunch I pulled it

off—slap, remove, straighten, repeat. But something was off, because while I had been so sure this was a milestone purchase, it turned out that I was just the same old me with a piece of fabric-wrapped metal around my wrist.

Confused, I sat in my bedroom looking at my wrist, trying to remember what exactly it was about this thing that I thought would be so life changing. It seemed silly now, and I was embarrassed by my own thoughts. Sure, I liked the bracelet, but it was a bracelet—nothing more, nothing less.

You're probably wise enough not to look for fulfillment in cheap jewelry, but perhaps your focus has just moved onto something else. We all struggle with that sense that if we could just get that one pair of shoes, have our kitchen remodeled, secure another promotion, we'd feel okay. We'd feel secure, valued, happy. And it's easy to see how this happens. We live in a culture where we're defined by what we can earn, achieve, consume. Our culture rewards and respects the quest and success of more, bigger, better. If we truly want to be happy, we'd better try our hardest to impress.

And then we can never stop trying. We can never stop accumulating, building, striving—because we won't feel secure and content until we have enough. But enough never comes. It doesn't matter what brand of clothing fills your closet, the model of your car, the address of your home, the title on your business card—it's not enough, and it will never be enough to settle your heart.

Friends, this is a defeating way to live. When we work so hard to buy the house we think will secure our identity, when we max out our credit card to get the look and style we hope will impress, when we run ourselves ragged so our children can be a part of every team, every opportunity, every Instagram photo op, we're surprised and disappointed to find that we don't feel any more secure, any more admired. We're still afraid and unsure, just with a little more "stuff" and a lot less energy.

But there's good news: we don't have to live that way. Because the message of the cross stands in stark contrast to the message of our culture. The message of the cross says you don't have to look for security in big houses and big bank accounts—you're already accepted as a child of God (1 John 3:1). The message of the cross says you don't have to keep up or impress in order to be loved—you're covered with perfect, eternal love (Ephesians 2:4–5). The message of the cross says you don't need to strive and sweat to get what you need— you'll find all your daily needs are met with God's generous provision (Matthew 6:26–30).

Yet the world won't hear it. Production, consumption, and accumulation seem to promise security, a life at ease. So it just seems foolish to choose a life that declines the rat race (1 Corinthians 1:18). But we know better. We know that while common thought suggests we fend for ourselves, we can only gain the confidence we're after when we trust in the Lord. Proverbs 3:5 encourages each one of us to "Trust in the Lord with all your heart and lean not on your own understanding." It's only then that we can find rest and quiet and peace within our souls.

Here are some of the questions we need to ask ourselves: *What am I after? How hard am I willing to push myself? Why am I working so hard for something I know I can't gain on my own? What will ever make me slow my pace? What's my break-ing point?*

Jon and I had found our breaking point. Could we now begin again, to rest in God's love and acceptance? Would we learn to stand confidently in the identity God created in us? We knew it was the only way forward—we were willing to try.

LOOKING INWARD: What's your slap bracelet? What are you striving for, working for, sweating for—in an attempt to feel secure? A bigger, better house? An impressive job title? Accomplished children? A flawless appearance? Why do you struggle to feel confident and secure?

LOOKING UPWARD: Spend a moment in silent meditation. Invite the Lord to highlight an area in your life where you're attempting to find value, stature, or security through your own efforts. Repent, ask for forgiveness, and ask for God's help in turning away from striving and toward trust.

LOOKING OUTWARD: Memorize Proverbs 3:5—it may already be familiar to you. This week, as you feel the cultural tug to earn more, get more, impress more (and you'll feel it—it's everywhere), repeat this verse.

Day 6

God-Story vs. Self-Story

This past spring our friends Jill and Guri secured a table at Talula's Table, one of the most difficult dinner reservations to snag in the entire country. There was seating for eight, and we were elated to accept their invitation to take two of those spots. About a month out, the restaurant emailed the menu and we immediately commenced drooling and dreaming. Spring vegetable fricassee sprinkled over goat's milk panna cotta with toasted honey wheat, popped sorghum, and local vinegar—that's just course one. We were in for several hours of delicious, inventive, inspired food.

On the night of the dinner, we arrived on the dot, not wanting to miss a single moment (or a single appetizer) and enjoyed four hours of food bliss. Small plates, glasses, and fun accompaniments arrived and were whisked away at just the right moments. We savored every course—olive oil poached halibut and bloomy cheeses with savory huckleberries and burnt honey (okay, back to drooling again). The dinner was creative, fresh, and maybe most importantly, nothing we could have cooked up on our own. It was truly special.

So much of food preparation these days is an opening of a package, a slapping together of a few too heavy or too sweet ingredients, a lack of finesse—this is true even in many restaurants. We aren't always accustomed to finding such care, such intentionality in a meal, or really much else in our culture. Our culture tends to aim for quick and efficient, for satisfying at the most surface level.

And it's so easy to fall in line with this way of life. We thoughtlessly bypass the best for the easiest, the instant gratification. We do this when we choose fad diets over a healthy lifestyle. We do this when we swipe our credit card for a cute new sweater. And we do this when we seek security and approval through what we can earn and accomplish.

Paul describes it this way in the book of Romans: "They pretended to know it all, but were illiterate regarding life. They traded the glory of God who holds the whole world in his hands for cheap figurines you can buy at any roadside stand" (Romans 1:22–23 MSG).

We do this all the time, don't we? Rather than trusting in God, "who holds the whole world in his hands," we place our hope in just about anything else. We may not have idols in our homes, but we certainly have our own cheap figurines. We place our faith in our appearance, our degrees and positions, in big houses, full closets, fancy vacations, and social status. But these trinkets won't save us—and chasing them robs so much of our energy, joy, and contentment.

In contrast, if we hold fast to God, he promises to rescue us, to put us right—secure, valued, at peace. Our energy won't be sapped and we'll reclaim our joy. In fact, Paul says that the person who is put right by trusting God "really lives" (Romans 1:16–17 MSG).

This is what it means to get what we really want, our deepest, truest desire—when we bypass the cheap knock-offs for the real thing. God is our Creator, Sustainer, the author of our lives. When he declares "this way is best," we should listen. We're foolish to trade out the Creator's best for the path of least resistance.

Our God relates to us with wisdom, intentionality, and great care. His desires for us are *for* us. He doesn't call us to anything just to make us jump, to beat us into submission. God isn't on a power trip. He invites us to trust him, to rest in him, to rely on him because as our Creator, he knows what's best. When we choose to rely on ourselves, working day and night, scrambling to get all we can, shuffling from event to team to practice to lesson, we are bound to run ourselves ragged.

God never intended for us to live this way. Paul writes that "if you go against the grain, you get splinters, regardless of which neighborhood you're from, what your parents taught you, what schools you attended" (Romans 2:9 MSG). This isn't about being punished, it's about natural consequences. When we rest in God's care, it brings about a healthy life, a full life. Whereas all that self-sufficient striving leaves us beat up.

Could it really be that easy? Let's release the pressure to succeed and receive the best life God has carefully crafted for us. God's promise to put us—and everything—right is based on him and his work. It's not based on what we do or

accomplish, or how perfect we try to be. "We call Abraham 'father' not because he got God's attention for living like a saint, but because God made something out of Abraham when he was a nobody" (Romans 4:17 MSG). He dared to trust God to do what only God could do.

Paul tells us that Abraham's extraordinary life is a God-story, not an Abraham-story (Romans 4:2 MSG). This idea applies to you and me too. I want to live an extraordinary life—but I've been going about it all wrong. I've been trying to secure my own place rather than resting in the one God's already made. I've been running myself ragged to create a life—ironically sapping the life right out of myself. It's time that I recognize my life as a God-story, not a Jen-story.

It's time to give up the striving and trust that our author and Creator knows best, desires the best, and will bring out the best in this story.

LOOKING INWARD: Have you been living a God-story or your own? What do you think are the key differences? Do you trust that God's desires for you are in your best interest? What makes you doubt that?

LOOKING UPWARD: Pray to God, committing your life as a God-story. Confess your doubts and fears, your striving and bent toward self-sufficiency. Acknowledge that his ways are the best ways—that his desires for you are *for* you. Thank him for his goodness, care, and intentionality in your life.

LOOKING OUTWARD: Draw two columns in a journal or on a scrap of paper. On the left, make a list of the signposts of a God-story. On the right, make a list of signposts of a self-story. Underneath, write a brief description of what this means for you, personally. Include specific actions or thoughts that might indicate that it's time for contemplation, confession, and recommitment.

Day 7

Sleeping in the Storm

I hid under the covers for an extra ten minutes, not ready to face the day. The same familiar dread weighed on me like it did every morning—*there's too much to do, I'll never make it, I should have gotten up an hour ago.*

Reluctantly, I reached for my phone on the bedside table. 11:30. How on earth could I have slept until 11:30? It seemed impossible. I was shuffling out of bed when it hit me. It was indeed 11:30. But it was 11:30 p.m. I slunk back into bed and laid awake, disoriented, doing my best to convince my body it was nighttime.

This was week one of our new bedtime.

It was doctor's orders, after all. He had quizzed Jon on our sleep patterns and quickly determined that we failed. Our usual bedtime landed around 2:00 a.m., and then we'd be up and moving just a few hours later. There was just so much to do. Going to bed felt irresponsible. If our eyes could stay open, so should our laptops.

The doctor didn't agree. No, it was not irresponsible to go to bed earlier. In fact, he told us that not only was our current schedule irresponsible, it was also wildly unhealthy. *Rude,* I thought. But desperate times and all. So early to bed we went.

And here, one week in, it was going so-so.

There were a few problems. To start with, I didn't want to go to bed early. I loved those late night hours because sometimes they were the only ones Jon and I spent together. I didn't care if we were both glued to our screens—we were in the same room and I was happy. When Jon would pipe up and say, "We should go to bed," I was instantly annoyed. But for the sake of his health, I'd pry myself out of my cozy white armchair and set my tea mug in the sink.

Another problem was the same thing that prompted me to wake up at 11:30 p.m. to start my day: our bodies weren't used to such luxurious amounts of rest. We'd trudge upstairs around 9:30 or 10 like real adults (and by that I mean it made us feel old) to get in bed. It just seemed so wrong. Some nights I'd fall asleep only to wake up disoriented a few hours later. Other nights I'd lay awake for hours feeling frustrated.

But the real problem, and the one that proved to be the most difficult to overcome, was that it felt counterintuitive to give up productive hours in order to reduce stress. How would we be healthier, happier, and breezier when our to-dos piled up and our inboxes overflowed? What advice did this doctor have for managing the impending chaos when we stopped putting in so much effort? Didn't he know that the world had problems to solve, we had causes to fight for, and there already wasn't enough time to do all that needed to be done?

As Christians, we're called to heal the world, care for the broken, love our family and neighbors, work to restore the earth, restore justice, and restore peace. We take it seriously.

And it's a big job. What we often forget, though, is that we're not called to do it all, and we're not called to do it alone. God doesn't ask or need us to save the world; he's got that covered—he asks us to come alongside his work, his movement, his efforts here. We're not asked to shoulder the burden of a broken world—we get to be a part of something beautiful and meaningful. We can do our part, and trust that an all-powerful God will hold the world in his perfect love.

In Luke 8, Jesus and the disciples set sail to spread the good news in a nearby city, and Jesus promptly falls asleep aboard the ship. A storm breaks out—Jesus keeps snoozing. When the disciples wake him in a panic, Jesus is less than impressed. After telling the storm to knock it off, he turns to the disciples and asks, "Where is your faith?" (v. 25). They didn't need to be worried—it was under control.

The ship arrives safely and when Jesus steps ashore he is immediately greeted by a naked, demon-possessed man shouting at him. After casting the demons into a herd of pigs he is then almost crushed by the clamoring crowd, heals a sick woman, and raises Jairus's daughter from the dead. I guess it's a good thing he got some rest, right?

Unfortunately, we're often not like Jesus, but much more like the disciples. We're afraid of the wind and waves of life. We're afraid we'll never meet our goals, we'll be knocked off course, fall short of our destination. So we panic and worry and scramble—all the while, Jesus rests soundly, knowing that God is in control.

When I picture the disciples frantic, scared for their lives, I know this is me lying in bed awake in a panic over all that is undone from the day, all that's before me tomorrow. The storm is swirling and there is no way I'm going to sleep through it. The Bible tells us to cast our cares on the Lord (1 Peter 5:7), but my middle-of-the-night prayers are less casting my cares and more clinging to them. As if my worrying alone will help everything be all right.

Yet Psalm 46 paints a bold picture of our God. He is "our refuge and strength, an ever-present help in trouble" (v. 1). He is here, with us, watching over this earth (v. 5). He breaks weapons and makes wars cease (v. 9). And he says to each of us, "Be still, and know that I am God" (v. 10).

It requires faith to close your laptop and go to bed when you're giving your all to a project you believe in. It takes faith to drop some activities to guarantee a solid night's sleep when you're not sure what the repercussions will be. It takes faith to snuggle into the covers while the outside world whirs and spirals and creaks and groans.

Let's choose to have faith, and get the rest our bodies and souls so desperately need. Let's follow Jesus's example, sleeping soundly in spite of the raging storm, because we know God is in control. And let's be still, because we know that he is God.

LOOKING INWARD: Do you struggle to get to bed at a healthy time? What keeps you from getting a full night's sleep? What is holding you back from making a change in this area?

LOOKING UPWARD: Consider Jesus asleep in the storm—ask God to help produce that kind of faith inside of you. Offer your worries and cares up to him, offer your schedule and to-dos up to him. Praise him that he is in control and can handle anything you're willing to release.

LOOKING OUTWARD: What is your normal rhythm of going to bed and getting up? How can you infuse more health into this practice? Perhaps go to bed an hour earlier, commit to not reading your phone in bed, set a consistent wake-up time. As a reminder, write "Be still and know that I am God" on a Post-it and stick it to your nightstand. Making a change like this isn't always easy—give it at least a couple weeks before making further adjustments.

Day 8

Frenzied Activism

One of my husband's common refrains is, "No more ideas." This is because one of my most common refrains is "I have a great idea."

According to Jon, it's not that my ideas aren't great—he says they are. (Thank you very much. I agree!) It's that I have too many of them. And I rarely have small ideas. And I will put them in motion. I will rally the troops. It may only take a half day from conception to fully planned.

Jon says it's too much.

I can't help it though. I see a need, I see a solution, and I'm happy to put in the work to make it happen. How could I stop having ideas, stop planning, organizing, inviting, when there is so much need everywhere I turn?

My brain doesn't discriminate by the size of the problem. We're talking large-scale community issues, neighborhood problems, or a friend in need. My mind instinctively fires off ideas. That new couple is struggling to meet friends? Let's throw a party! There's little faith and discipleship community for our kids? Let's start an area-wide organization! The

students at a nearby elementary school are struggling emotionally, academically? Let's enlist and train lunch mentors
from the community!

It seems wrong not to act on these ideas when I know
I'm capable, and I know it's addressing a real problem. Jon
is right in a way, though: it can be too much. When I get
too many great ideas running at once, it's not all that great.
I'm exhausted. I'm overextended. I'm terse with my family (or
so I'm told). Still, how could I pass up something that could
help? The world is so broken. How could I relax when there's
so much work to do?

The problem is that while we think rest and breaks
are unhelpful, our overwork is actually counterintuitive to
our quest for peace, for a healed and whole world. Thomas
Merton explains it this way: "There is a pervasive form of
contemporary violence to which the idealist . . . most easily
succumbs: activism and overwork. The rush and pressure of
modern life are a form, perhaps the most common form, of
its innate violence. To allow oneself to be carried away by a
multitude of conflicting concerns, to surrender to too many
demands, to commit oneself to too many projects, to want to
help everyone in everything, is to succumb to violence. . . .
The frenzy of [our activism] neutralizes [our] work for peace.
It destroys [our] own inner capacity for peace. It destroys the
fruitfulness of [our] own work, because it kills the root of
inner wisdom which makes work fruitful."[1]

Sobering words, yes?

It's not noble to spend yourself. You're not a better person because you've completely worn yourself out serving at
church and volunteering in your community. You don't earn

bonus points for joining in on more causes, trying to fix more problems, at the expense of your own soul. This type of over-work is a violence to ourselves—it robs our peace. And it makes us ineffective. Run-down and on edge, we're achieving the opposite of peace. And when our hearts are in turmoil, that's exactly what we're pouring out to those around us.

While we are invited into God's restorative work here on this earth (Matthew 28:16–20), we are also given a pretty straightforward command to rest as well (Exodus 20:8–11). And if we're worried about the irresponsibility of resting while the world churns, we can look to the example of God himself. Because immediately after setting the world to motion, God—who loves the world and cares more than we ever could—takes a break. He rests.

Genesis 2 opens: "Thus the heavens and the earth were completed in all their vast array. By the seventh day God had finished the work he had been doing; so on the seventh day he rested from all his work. Then God blessed the seventh day and made it holy, because on it he rested from all the work of creating that he had done" (vv. 1–3).

In his inspiring book, *Sabbath as Resistance*, theologian Walter Brueggemann takes a closer look at that first Sabbath rest, saying, "That divine rest on the seventh day of creation has made clear that (a) YHWH is not a workaholic, (b) that YHWH is not anxious about the full functioning of creation, and (c) that the well-being of creation does not depend on endless work."[2]

The restoration of this world is not dependent on our ability to push through, work endlessly. Yes, needs abound. There is struggle, disparity, loneliness, abuse, poverty, sickness, and

strife at almost every angle, if we have eyes to see it. Yet we can, and are called to, rest. We can, and are called to, trust that God is in control. We can, and are called to, release the burden we were never intended to bear.

No matter how good our intentions, overwork takes its toll. It's easier to deride the kind of overwork that means extra office hours, taking a call from the boss on the weekend, or responding to emails at the dinner table. But when the work is good, meaningful, helping the world, we're much more likely to keep plugging along in spite of our depleted state.

But if we believe that God loves us, that he wants the best for us, this must extend to our mental, emotional, and physical health as well. This is why Psalm 127:2 tells us that God grants sleep to those he loves. And this is why God invites us to regular rhythms of rest and refreshment. In the book of Mark, after being confronted by the Pharisees, Jesus boldly declares, "The Sabbath was made for man, not man for the Sabbath" (Mark 2:27). The Sabbath isn't intended to restrict and restrain us—it's a gift that offers us two things we desperately need: rhythms of rest, and an opportunity to express a deep trust in God's promises to heal our world, to set things right.

The gift of the Sabbath means that while we are called to God's mission, that includes both rhythms of work and rhythms of rest. The gift of the Sabbath means that the fate of the world is in God's hands, not ours. The gift of the Sabbath means that while the world is at war, we can still be at peace.

LOOKING INWARD: Do you easily succumb to "activism and overwork"? Do you struggle to be at peace in a world that is raging? Which problems plague your heart and mind? How have you balanced your involvement, time, and energy in these areas?

LOOKING UPWARD: Praise God for the way he loves us as whole people—body, mind, and soul. Thank him for his gift of the Sabbath, his call to rest, his power to hold the weight of the world so we don't have to. Confess the ways you fail to trust him and fall into anxiety and overwork, and hold your hands open, offering up the jumbled mess of this world to him—to his heart, his power, and his healing work.

LOOKING OUTWARD: We are often quick to act, preferring the concreteness of a project over prayer. Yet we can't solve every problem or fill every need. Let's learn to trust in God's restorative work. Write out a prayer for God's work to be done, for the world to be healed, restored. Allow this prayer to become a regular practice—perhaps part of your morning routine as you head out into the world, or maybe as you encounter needs throughout your day.

Day 9

Scrambling for Manna

We'd begun to make significant changes to our lifestyle after Jon's diagnosis, but there was one area we were particularly reluctant to heed the doctor's advice: his job.

Jon had worked in churches for over a decade. Some of these churches are beautiful expressions of the Christian family, and I am grateful for the way they proclaim God's love, serve as the hands and feet of Jesus, and live by the Holy Spirit. Yet churches can also be political, corporate, grandstanding, and deeply wounding. And churches can, on occasion, devour their own. (Hey, here's a free tip: Be kinder to your pastor. And your pastor's family.)

After a few painful experiences we were banged up—yet being ever willing to press on, we'd done just that, pressed on. We thought we were being strong, but in reality our pace didn't allow our wounds to heal.

We knew that church work was a significant source of stress. We knew he was running himself into the ground. We knew that he needed to let it go. But it felt sad—because we were dedicated, we cared, we loved our church. And it felt risky—because it was all we had ever known.

But after a few months of watching his progress zapped by circumstances at work, we couldn't ignore the sinking feeling that his doctor was right. To de-stress and get healthy, Jon would need to step away from his job, he'd need to work less hours, he'd need space to heal and process.

So, after a year plus of hobbling along and dealing with pain, sadness, and worry, Jon left his steady, sure-thing, full-time job. He took what was previously a creative outlet and grew it into a business—and we launched further into the unknown.

When you embark on a new project, especially one which your family's livelihood and security depend upon, the pressure is high. You'd better work hard, work long, make every moment count, give everything you've got. Everything is riding on this.

Except your health, which is riding on rhythms of rest, breathing room, time to process, space to hear God's voice, exercise, sleep, and recreation.

You see the tension, yes?

Thankfully, Jon's business launched well and drew clients quickly. We all survived. Still, this dynamic was a real struggle in that early stage. When your entire family is relying on your ability to secure contracts and build a network, it's pretty tough to close the laptop and get a good night's sleep. And it's even more difficult to take a three-day weekend to recharge. There's always a temptation to get right to work when you wake at 5:00 a.m. rather than heading to the gym.

How can you rest, take a break, when you're starting at zero, have nothing to fall back on, and you're hanging out in unknown territory? It feels irresponsible to enjoy a leisurely walk after breakfast when you're not sure you'll be able to pay your bills in six months.

I have to wonder if this is how the Israelites felt when they left Egypt. God miraculously freed them from oppression and provided Moses to lead them to a new land. But after two months in a desert, they were hangry, frustrated, and just done (Exodus 16). Even death by the Egyptians sounded better than their current desert wanderings. But as he always does, God heard their cries, and every morning he sent manna, food from heaven. How beautiful is that?

There were some stipulations though. They were only to collect enough for each day—no stockpiling. God would provide what they needed, when they needed it. And there was to be no work on the Sabbath—on the sixth day they could collect double in preparation for a day of rest.

This may sound simple, until you place yourself in their sandals. The Israelites have been traversing the desert for over two months with very limited resources. When all hope feels lost, when dying sounds preferable to this version of living, food literally rains from the sky. These are real people, with real appetites, and real families to feed. It's easy to judge when we read of them trying to hoard the manna (v. 20) or heading out on the Sabbath to collect more (v. 27), but their circumstances and past experiences were loud voices calling, "Hurry! Get out there! Save yourself! You could starve—you don't know what tomorrow will bring!"

We hear those voices too, don't we? We all have our own past experiences that beckon us to worry, scramble—that tell us we're foolish not to do everything we can to take care of ourselves.

I don't think God is one to get into a shouting match—but if we have ears to hear trust over fear, peace over worry, provision over striving, there's a still, small voice inviting us to faith, to resting in him, to receiving what he's poised to give. Fear shouts and intimidates, but trust gently invites us into his arms.

Even when we're in the wilderness, even when resources are scarce, God mandates Sabbath rest for his people.[3] The Israelites would be cared for day by day, and so will we. We don't need to be fearful of getting enough and having enough, because we have a good God who cares for us if we'll let him. We can, even when the future feels unknown, live in the rhythms of rest that both our bodies and souls need.

LOOKING INWARD: Do fear and scarcity ever get the best of you? Why is it so much easier to listen to fear, than trust? What do you fear?

LOOKING UPWARD: Confess to God the ways you doubt his care, listen to other voices over his, and fall into rhythms of striving. Thank him for his gift of rest and his consistent love and provision. Ask him to continue leading you into trust over fear.

LOOKING OUTWARD: Choose one day this week to practice Sabbath rest. Commit to not working. When fear creeps in, offer up a prayer of trust and thanksgiving.

Day 10

Busy Lemmings

I hate to let you down, but I am that person who walks into street signs while texting. I know, I'm the picture of elegance. Yet even more alarming is that—on more than one occasion—I've been almost run over while pecking away at my phone. Somehow the crowds on the sidewalk lull me into a false sense of security as I bounce around the city between appointments. If everyone is walking in the direction of my favorite coffee shop and I'm craving an Americano, I just fall in line with the crowd and take advantage of not really having to pay attention.

I can walk several blocks with my head down, scrolling through texts and responding to emails, because I'm right in the mix of everyone else. Surely all of these people would stop if the light was red. Surely they wouldn't just walk right out into oncoming traffic. These seem like safe assumptions—but unfortunately, they are not, and I receive a startling reminder of this once or twice a year.

There's just something so comfortable about fitting in, being right in the middle of the crowd. It feels safe, known.

We can easily trick ourselves into thinking that if everyone else is doing it, it must be a fine and normal way to proceed.

Yet it doesn't necessarily work out that way, does it? Whenever we hear of presumably good-natured teenagers participating in some sort of heinous act it's almost always blamed on herd mentality. It's the fraternity hazing that goes too far. The straight-laced girl who ends up in the hospital after an underage party. It's whenever someone follows suit, joining in a behavior without thought, simply because it's what everyone is doing.

We see these stories on the news and shake our heads and wonder what is wrong with the world today. Yet we fall into this pattern too. We structure our homes, our finances, our families, and our lives based on our sense of the cultural norm in our communities—without thought.

That's what Jon and I had done. We'd shaped our family calendar and rhythm by simply signing up for the things everyone else does. With our two sons, Ellington and Breckin, both in late elementary school, our family schedule was in full tilt. It was completely normal for us to be busy every night with music lessons and sports teams and after-school clubs, just as it was completely normal for almost every other family we knew.

This is, after all, what it means to raise children in today's world. You seize every opportunity you can for them. You drive them to activities every evening so they can grow and excel. You take them to school early and you maximize the weekends. You plan playdates and volunteer in their classroom for elementary-aged networking. This is how we parent today. And I sure was doing my best.

But something bothered me. For all the wonderful activities and groups and experiences that saturated our children's weeks, they sure didn't seem very happy about it. I mean, yes, they enjoyed the teams and the clubs and the lessons enough—but by the end of each day, they weren't just tired, they were drained, dimmer. I started wondering if maybe all these activities that were crafted to make our kids the best were sapping their ability to be themselves.

I began whittling down their commitments and noticed a difference. As the next season approached, I made some tough calls and only registered them for a couple activities each. They seemed relieved. Jon seemed relieved. I was definitely relieved.

But remember as a kid when we wanted to do something our parents didn't approve of, we'd argue that everyone else was doing it? The typical response would be, "If everyone jumped off a cliff, would you do it too?" And now in my mid-thirties I can tell you that apparently my answer is yes, yes I would.

Because as fall drew near, I grew nervous. Our boys were set for a reasonable, healthy pace. However, a healthy pace isn't what is valued in our culture. What is valued is winning, and crushing it, and Ivy League schools, and travel teams, and first chairs, and honors classes, and future CEOs. If your children aren't simultaneously a part of an after-school club, a serious sports team, music lessons, and tutoring, you may as well start converting your basement into an apartment, because that is where they're headed.

With every conversation where I learned that little Johnny has swim three days, a writing tutor twice a week,

travel soccer all weekend, and cotillion after school, I edged a little closer to the cliff. Maybe I should check out those after-school programs again. Maybe we can squeeze in an extra tennis lesson once a week. It would just be irresponsible to not give the boys an edge.

Just like that, I jumped. And we all paid the price.

As parents, we set the tone for our families. We choose the pace and rhythm we want. We determine who we take our cues from. We have a responsibility to do so with intentionality. Do we thoughtlessly fall in line with the crowd, heads down as we walk toward sure disaster? Or do we lift our eyes and listen to the voice of the One who longs to see us healthy and whole?

The crowd tells us that we need to hustle and scrape and strive to get what we need, to secure our spot. Jesus tells us to seek him first, and the rest will fall in place (Matthew 6:32–33). The trouble is that there is no neutral—we have to make a conscious choice. We'll have to take the phones out of our faces and turn our brains back on, friends, because when we don't choose to follow Jesus, we've already made a decision to follow the crowd.

In Romans 12:2, Paul reminds us to "not conform to the pattern of this world, but be transformed by the renewing of your mind. Then you will be able to test and approve what God's will is—his good, pleasing and perfect will." Eugene Peterson paraphrases it this way: "Don't become so well-adjusted to your culture that you fit into it without even thinking. Instead, fix your attention on God. You'll be changed from the inside out. Unlike the culture around you, always dragging you down to its level of immaturity, God

brings the best out of you, develops well-formed maturity in you" (MSG).

When we choose to follow Jesus, to fix our eyes on him, it reshapes our view of ourselves, God, and our world. Our outlook and mind-set are renewed with a fresh understanding of God's love, his power, his sovereignty, his goodness. Suddenly, that bustling and hurrying and climbing all seems unnecessary. Foolish, even.

Do you remember the old computer game, Lemmings? I loved trying to move obstacles and break barriers in order for my line of little Lemmings to make it safely to their destination. It was tricky, because if the first Lemming took a wrong turn, the second would follow, and so on until the entire string was headed in the wrong direction. Similarly, if you weren't fast enough, the entire string would walk straight off a cliff— one after the other, each steadily stepping off into the abyss.

It is so easy to be formed by the patterns of the world. It is so easy to become so well adjusted to our culture that we fit in without even thinking. It's so easy to keep our heads down and follow a line of lemmings straight off a cliff or into oncoming traffic.

When Jon's doctor questioned our lifestyle, I had bristled. We held down jobs. We ate healthy food. We took care of our children. Our house was clean. We did not live some rock-and-roll lifestyle. As far as I could tell, we lived most of our days and weeks like anyone else.

But maybe that was the problem.

Maybe we're all caught in this cycle. Maybe we're all plodding along this path of least resistance, lulled by the crowd into an easy, apathetic approach that says, "this is just how

things are." We're overscheduling ourselves and our families in an effort to keep up. Our bodies, souls, and relationships are running on fumes. We're living just like everyone else.

But we don't have to. There's a better way, a brighter way.

Let's kick mediocrity to the curb—who wants to be ordinary anyhow? And let's lift our eyes, fix our gaze, and renew our minds. Because we're really made for so much more than cliff jumping.

LOOKING INWARD: What cultural expectations are placed on you and your family? In what ways do you feel pressured to do more, attend more, be more? Is it difficult for you to set your eyes on Jesus rather than be lulled by the crowd?

LOOKING UPWARD: Praise God for his transforming work in our lives. Invite him to renew your mind and commit to keeping your eyes fixed on him.

LOOKING OUTWARD: What cultural values, activities, or pressures do you need to shed? What is one tangible way you can make a stand today?

Day 11

Baby Wisdom

If you've ever had a baby of your own, or one in your care, you've played the fun game of "why are you crying?" It's a blast. You get to scramble and panic and try everything in your soothe-the-baby arsenal, all to the nerve-grinding soundtrack of unfettered, uninhibited screaming. What fun!

It's not until you're around a baby that you realize how much a human being is affected by her physical needs. When my boys were born, it became quickly evident that every part of our lives revolved around their need to eat, sleep, stretch out, move, rest. It was serious business.

When Ellington, our oldest, was just a few months old, I noticed that he would get fussy around 4:30 every single afternoon. I'd spend the tail end of the afternoon trying to keep him happy, then Jon would do his best for a couple hours until bedtime, sweet bedtime, graced us. One day, worn out on this routine, I fed Ellington at 4:00 p.m. and popped him in bed. It felt odd, but I was desperate to avoid the meltdown. I figured we'd pay for it later when he was up all night—torture, but at least a different form. But he slept through

until the next morning. When we awoke, refreshed, it hit us: he wasn't just being fussy—he was tired. At 4:30 in the afternoon. All that daily crabbing and crying was his baby version of begging to go to bed.

We soon discovered that he was also happier with a long morning nap as well. So, for the next couple years, he napped from 9:30 a.m. to 1:00 p.m., then went to bed at 4:30 p.m. until 6:00 a.m. the next morning. If you're keeping track, that means he was awake seven hours per day. Sounds crazy, I know, but with all that sleep, he quickly became the happiest little guy around. When Breckin was born, he gladly joined the same rhythm, and the two of them slept like little hibernating bear cubs.

Looking back, I wish Jon and I had taken some cues from them—their baby wisdom could have done wonders for us. Sadly, while we all start with an innate understanding of our body's needs, we seem to train ourselves to ignore them. As we grow older, we hear the message loud and clear that we need to power through and toughen up. "Not needing sleep" and "skipping breakfast" are badges of honor. After all, you can get so much more done if you don't waste time on pesky things like eating, sleeping, and exercise. I think we all know deep down that it doesn't really work that way—but we sure try.

The thing is, our bodies weren't meant to operate on empty. When we don't take care of them, we can expect trouble. We may think we're getting by, or even getting ahead, but we're fooling ourselves. All that misuse and lack of care is going to show up whether we acknowledge it or not. In our health, our relationships, our lack of patience, our attitude.

As our babies turned into toddlers they would occasionally be crabby, or not listen well, whine, or become overly

frustrated—shocking, I know. More often than not, after a quick reflection on the day, I'd know exactly what was going on: they'd missed a snack, we were running late on dinner, they'd been up later than normal the night before, or cooped up all day. Their little bodies were running on steam.

"You're just hungry," I'd say, fishing around in my bag for a snack. It's incredible what a handful of almonds or a granola bar can do for one's outlook. I know this mostly from personal experience because I suffer from a condition known as being hangry. Or maybe it's my husband who suffers from my condition—because I can tell you, I am really not someone you want to be around if I miss a meal or snack time (yes, my kids are old and in school all day but I've really embraced that whole snack time concept). To be safe, just don't ride home from church with me. Our church lets out late on Sundays, and by the time we've chatted and gotten in the car I hit panic-level hunger.

"What do you want to do for lunch?" Jon usually asks me on the drive home.

"I can't make these decisions! Why would you ask me that? Do I have to do everything? I can't even think straight! I'm going to pass out! Or vomit! Just get me to food! Any food! As fast as possible! And don't make me answer any more questions!" I reply.

It's taken years of Jon ~~rudely~~ helpfully pointing out this pattern for me to grasp how affected I am by a lack of food.

It's more than food, though. Babies lose their minds when they are hungry, but they also lose their minds when they need sleep, or when they need activity, or when they need

quiet. And I hate to be the bearer of bad news, but we're all essentially just grown-up babies. Our bodies need nourishment, sleep, and exercise to function properly. These are the basic building blocks of our physical health—and our emotional health too. Because when our blood sugar plummets, we've stayed up all night, or we haven't gotten our heart rates up, we just feel off.

On more than one occasion, I've said to a child, "I know you're tired, but that's no excuse to be unkind." On more than one occasion, I should have said this to myself. But when it's me who's exhausted and rude, I'm much more likely to place the blame on the other person, of course. When I'm irritated, surely the problem is the person who used the last slice of bread, leaving me with a toast-less avocado toast—not me, who got four hours of sleep for the past week.

Whether we want to admit it or not, we're at our weakest when we're depleted. It's no coincidence that Satan's temptation of Christ comes after forty days of fasting, when Matthew describes Jesus as "hungry" (Matthew 4:1–2). Of course this is when temptation strikes—another key moment would be if Jesus had a newborn and hadn't slept through the night for three months. Or if he had been stuck at a desk for twelve hours straight. Anytime our body becomes unbalanced, so does our ability to think clearly, make wise choices, and exercise self-control.

It's time that we go back to the basics. It's time that we attend to our own needs. It's time that we stop powering through, and drop the notion that it's tougher, better, more admirable to sacrifice our health for a chance at success.

LOOKING INWARD: What are your body's signs to indicate it's depleted? Do you become overly sensitive? Do you feel scattered and unable to focus? Shaky or irritable? Identify these signs. What is your body trying to tell you? What patterns do you notice? In what area is your body asking for more care?

LOOKING UPWARD: Praise God that you are wonderfully made, that his work is wonderful (Psalm 139:14). Confess the ways you mistreat your body—his creation. Commit to him your intention to care for yourself well, to bring health and balance back to your life.

LOOKING OUTWARD: What is one way you can step further into health, into caring for your body? Maybe you'll go for a walk after dinner each night. Maybe you'll begin packing a lunch to ensure you eat during the work day. Maybe you'll go to bed a half hour earlier. Choose one tangible step, and notice the way your body responds to the gift you offer.

Day 12

Leaving the Mess

When our boys were two and four years old, I made a decision that would haunt me for years to come. It was a Saturday morning and we'd cooked up a big pancake breakfast for the kids—chocolate chip pancakes, bowls full of fresh berries, fresh squeezed OJ. It was all their favorites and an enormous mess.

Normally, as soon as they darted from the table I would scurry around cleaning up—who wants to spend the rest of the day with pancake spatters and syrupy plates? But the kids were flying high with excitement, all four of us were in our pajamas, goofing around, enjoying a morning at home together, and I thought, for the first time ever, *Leave the mess. Enjoy the morning together—don't be so uptight.*

And so I left the mess. I told myself it was fine. I was going to be laid-back now.

We chased the giggling kids upstairs. They ran around singing, screaming, laughing. We laughed. I congratulated myself on such amazing growth—here we were watching a toddler circus when right below us in the kitchen it looked like a breakfast bomb had detonated.

I ran downstairs for a refresh on coffee and that's when I saw it: a beautiful basket of lemons sitting on our counter. I froze. My stomach sunk. Someone had been in our house.

There was a note from a neighbor we hadn't yet met. They had been away at their second home in California, and now that they had returned, they wanted to welcome us to the neighborhood. I looked at this beautiful, picturesque basket of cheerful lemons—sitting in the midst of a greasy griddle, drips of batter, berry remnants on a cutting board, glasses with orange pulp now glued to the insides. I couldn't fathom this woman bringing her hand-picked lemons into this scene, this proper and polite stranger standing in such a room. And I knew that I would never, ever leave a mess in the kitchen again.

And I haven't.

My valiant effort to be a little more laid-back had back-fired, playing right into my inner monologue prompting me to *do it all, do it perfectly, hold it all together, leave no messes, make no mistakes.*

And I couldn't let it go.

Even years later, knowing what the doctor had said—that we needed to relax—knowing it was true, it still felt so wrong. I felt constant pressure. Do you feel it too? How could we rest? We have all this work to do. There are so many messes. The world is a mess, our community is a mess, our families are a mess—we ourselves are a mess.

A quick peek into the Gospels tells us this isn't the Jesus way, though. In Mark 6, Jesus calls the twelve disciples and sends them out in pairs traveling, preaching, healing, and anointing. In verses 30–31, they return to Jesus, reporting all they've seen and done. And here is where it gets interesting.

Jesus invites the disciples to come away, get some rest, and recover from their work. He doesn't say, "Great! Now head back out and double your speed—there are a lot of sick to heal. And find a way to expedite the anointing process now that you've got that down. While you're at it, could you reorganize our supplies? You're obviously really on top of things."

I'm sure most of us have encountered that type of response. "You're done? Awesome. Now do this too!" Whether we're working for a company, volunteering for a local organization, or helping a family member, hard work and a job well done is usually met with more work.

We're not quick to let ourselves off the hook either. When is the last time that you finished a project, reorganized a closet, or helped a neighbor in need, and didn't feel an instant internal pressure to do more, help again, or further your reach?

For those of us who are perfectionists, this is a monumental challenge. In terms of my home, it doesn't matter how tired I am or what kind of day I've had, I will not sit down and relax at night until everything is just right. If there's a dish in the sink, a stray sock on the living room floor, or laundry to be started, there is no way I'm going to settle in with a book and a mug of tea. And I can promise you I've never again left a breakfast mess sit. My (annoying) saying is, "Why wait 'til later when I could just do it now?" What this really means is that I'm unable to relax when I know there's more work to be done.

Now apparently—and I know you'll be as shocked to discover this as I was—there are some people who can relax even with a stray sock on the rug. It's ludicrous, right? But these people are onto something. Because learning to stop

and rest may not have huge implications on your housekeeping, but learning to do so could very well reshape the way we structure our days and our hearts.

When Jesus called the disciples away to rest and refresh, it wasn't because the world was problem free. And it wasn't because he didn't care enough. It was because he was acutely aware of two key elements at play: what it means to be human, and the perfect, unstoppable plan of God. Being both fully God and fully human (Philippians 2:6–8), Jesus knew firsthand our needs for rest and replenishment. He knew firsthand the power and promise of God to see this thing through, set this world right—and he knew that it isn't dependent on our constant toiling.

If we're walking with Jesus, we don't need to save the world, because he's already got that covered. And while we're invited into his mission, we need to give ourselves, and others, permission to follow his lead and take a break. Slip away. Recover and refresh. Is there more work to be done? Of course. Are more demands and requests coming your way? Always. But we can follow Jesus's path here, trusting and resting in God's power and promise to see us through. So please, come away and rest.

LOOKING INWARD: In what ways are you trying to carry the problems and needs of the world? How does your lack of trust drive your inability to rest? What would it look like to trust in God's promise to you, to this world, to setting things right?

LOOKING UPWARD: Confess to God your lack of trust in him, his timing, his plan. Praise God that he is the One who will make things right, restore our world, and heal every heart. Commit to following Jesus in both matters of serving and of resting. In working, healing, and ministering, and in being refreshed.

LOOKING OUTWARD: Where are you putting in work and effort based on a lack of trust? Prayerfully consider what commitment, activity, or responsibility you need to release. Declare your trust in God's promises, and cross this item off your to-do list without worry.

Day 13

Overdrawn

I've only bounced a check once. It was a decade ago, but I still feel an inner "ouch" when I think of it. Maybe this sounds a little uptight to you, but my distinct impression growing up was that bouncing a check was serious business. Seriously wrong. Seriously embarrassing. And a serious no-no. So imagine my horror when I realized that I had not only sent out a bad check, but I had sent it to someone I knew. Double ouch.

We were living in Chicago at the time, preparing for a cross-country move, when I noticed on Facebook that Travis, a casual friend from college, was roasting his own coffee beans. Totally fascinating. I sent him a message asking for a recommendation on a roaster, and he wrote back saying he was upgrading his roaster and would be happy to sell the beginner model he'd been using.

Great—sure. After all, why go all out when you're just giving it a try? I popped a check in the mail and looked forward to home-roasted beans.

A week or so later, my husband mentioned in passing that he had gone ahead and opened bank accounts with the new

bank we'd be using out west. Great—sure. I love when people are proactive.

Except, after a few hours passed, I realized that all direct payments had already been diverted to the new accounts. And that over the past couple weeks I had still been spending money out of our old account (note to friends in the early years of marriage—communication is key).

I instantly felt ill. I had committed the unforgivable sin—I had sent a check that linked to a defunct account. I have a feeling that this was not as devastating for Travis. I was mortified—he was, I would later learn, in the midst of launching a now massively successful new coffee company. I still cannot see a bag of their coffee beans without my stomach flipping. On the other hand, he, I assume, has moved on.

Unfortunately, no matter your intentions, or how much money you earn, you can't keep drawing from an account you're not refilling. And this goes for more than your bank account. We can't expect a friend to keep offering favors if we never give into the relationship. We can't expect our car to run without stopping at a gas station (one lesson I haven't quite taken to heart yet). And we can't keep giving of ourselves if we aren't being poured back into. Yet that is exactly what I tried to do.

I was giving everything I had—taking care of my own responsibilities, extra ones Jon had to release, trying to keep everyone's spirits up even though my own were shaky, trying to keep all balls in the air so that we could pretend Jon's illness wasn't rocking our world. If I was honest with myself, I was totally depleted. And in all of this scurrying, I had let go of the only things that could have refilled me.

Life-giving practices are the regular parts of our lifestyle that help us be whole—things that tune our hearts to what is good and true. Life-giving practices remind us of what we believe deep down, even when it's way deep down. Life-giving practices restore our weary hearts so they can beat strong again. We need these things to stay grounded, clear-eyed, and steady. We need them to retain our joy. And in a swirl of chaos and despair, I had slowly let go of everything I should have held on to. I needed to make a change.

I started out by heading to the gym. In the midst of stress and to-dos and being completely overwhelmed, this had been one of the first things to slip through the cracks. I rationalized it by telling myself that by skipping the gym, I was saving time in my day, thus relieving pressure. And couldn't I catch back up later once life had calmed down? What was the worst that could happen, I'd put on a few extra pounds?

Somehow, I had deceived myself into thinking that an hour of exercise was simply about my physical health, when in reality it had a significant impact on my emotional health as well. One unimpressive workout later, I had so much more than sore muscles—I felt renewed, refocused, and for the first time in a while, reenergized.

Later that week, I forced myself to sit down with a journal. Full disclosure: the first day I didn't write a thing. I just sat, pen in hand, staring off. But the next day, I sat down again and a few words came. In time, the floodgates opened and all sorts of thoughts and feelings and emotions came pouring out as the most honest prayer. It wasn't pretty, but it didn't have to be.

Authentic prayer is less about honesty with God (he already knows) and more about being honest with ourselves. I was surprised to discover the intensity of what was going on inside. It hurt to feel those feelings—but it was so good to let them out, to release their hold over me, and to ask God to make sense of it all.

Also, I realized I needed to set aside some time for friends and family. I needed to reach out, reengage, and spend time with all those good people in life who speak words of truth, peace, and care. You know who I mean: The people who help you laugh and make it okay to cry. People who show up just to share a meal, reminding you that you're not alone, not the only one with bumps in their road, that there are still, and always, blessings along the path.

We simply cannot keep giving what we do not have. And even on our very best days or most stress-free weeks, we need these life-giving practices. Because not only do they save us from bottoming out during the storms, they keep our hearts humble, gentle, and joyful when everything is smooth sailing.

Some of these practices are as simple as eating dinner as a family or ditching your phone on Saturday mornings. Maybe it's a morning walk with time to pray and reflect. Or perhaps you have a standing coffee date with a trusted mentor. While life-giving practices may look different for each one of us, the result is the same: a life that is centered, alive, rooted in hope, and never running dry.

LOOKING INWARD: What refills you? What practices restore life and keep hope alive? Consider your energy, emotional health, and schedule—do you have adequate life-giving practices as a regular part of your rhythm? What practices have you let go of that you wish you hadn't?

LOOKING UPWARD: Ask the Lord to illuminate the ways you are depleted. Thank him for seeing into your heart, understanding you better than you understand yourself. Thank him for the ways he refills you, restores you. Open your hands to his gift of refreshment. Listen for his voice, leading you toward health and wholeness.

LOOKING OUTWARD: Don't wait another day to begin restoring health. Commit time in the next twenty-four hours to being refilled. Set up a coffee date with a trusted friend, head out for a run, take a nap on your porch.

Day 14

More Than a Meal

"Bring the boys and come for dinner." This is a text I received countless times from my friend Christie as Jon began to travel regularly for his new company. It was a delicate time for us—we were still dealing with wounds from the past, yet having to trudge full steam ahead into our future. We were happy and sad, relieved and stressed, energized and exhausted, all at once. And Christie knew it.

Christie and I moved to the same street the same summer a few years back and became instant friends. Having almost zero green space on our block means the kids all play in the street together—a roaming pack of children from toddler through elementary school. It's quite a scene.

As it turns out, a by-product of being forced to spend all of your outdoor time in the street with your neighbors is that it only takes a couple months for someone to feel like family. And that's exactly what happened.

Just like good family, Christie instinctively reached out whenever she knew I could use the support. Jon's traveling?

Come for dinner. You're on your own all week? Let's share dessert on the patio after the kids go to bed.

Sometimes when the boys and I would crash their family dinner I felt a little guilty. After all, Christie had two young kids at home, she was coaching a lacrosse team out of state, her husband often worked late, and here she was prepping and cooking and cleaning up for us. Shouldn't I be taking care of myself? Yet I couldn't deny that through her offering, I was receiving way more than an occasional (delicious) meal—I was receiving support, understanding, friendship, and the incredible gift of knowing you're not alone, never forgotten.

It was a lesson I had begun to learn the previous year when we were in the throes of the unknown. Jon's pain levels and medical complications worsened by the week. We had no reprieve, no answers, and almost no hope. Yet I continued to decline offers for help. Technically, I could handle it myself. Why bother people? And I thought, worst-case scenario, we order takeout. We won't starve.

Yet as the heavy days turned into heavy weeks, and those weeks accumulated into months, I began to wear out. I received an email from Nanette—a friend, an elder at our church, and a woman the rest of us admire with awe. She said, "I'm bringing a meal. You can't say no. Let me know when to stop by." And that was that. She brought the meal (really, multiple meals all in one big bag), and as she drove away, I stared at this gracious, beautiful meal, now unpacked on my countertop, and just cried.

Then, I heard from Lauren. And then they pulled together a few more friends and brought us meals for weeks. All these grace-filled, healthy, beautiful meals. Each time, my heart was overwhelmed, and each time, I cried over their sweet offering.

Maybe this is why Jesus describes himself as the Bread of Life, broken for us. And maybe this—cooking and serving and feasting and sharing—is one way we model his love and pass it on to those around us. Because when we offer ourselves to nourish the bodies and souls of another, it is more than just meal delivery. When we wash and chop and roast and whisk, it's more than just putting dinner on the table—it's pouring our lives into someone else.

Yet, it's so much easier to pour ourselves out than it is to receive life from others. I love cooking for my family, hosting friends and neighbors, bringing new people together around a good meal. I don't even mind the cleanup, because it's a sign of a full night and full hearts. But sometimes, caring for ourselves means allowing others to care for us. Sometimes we need to simply show up and partake, open our door and receive a meal. Sometimes we need to let someone run our errands, watch our children, or sit quietly next to us while we cry.

The problem is that, whether we can admit it or not, each of us harbors some level of sinful pride. We want to be able to solve our own problems and take care of ourselves. We want to be invincible and strong. We feel so good when we can at least maintain a facade of having everything under control. But friends, this is no way to live.

I tend to be quite organized. I can accomplish a lot in a day. My parents raised me to be capable and a hard worker. I have a lot of energy for the projects and people I care about. So admitting that I can't do it—that I need help—that I'm struggling, it's really difficult. It takes a swipe at my identity.

But Proverbs 16:18 says, "Pride goes before destruction, a haughty spirit before a fall," and I think it goes even further than that. Because pride is also what keeps us on the ground. When we cling to our "I've got this" attitude, we can't help ourselves back up—and neither can anyone else.

But we don't have to stay there—on the ground with a bruised ego, too proud to ask for help. James 4:10 tells us, "Humble yourselves before the Lord, and he will lift you up." When we're able to let go of our pride and admit that we need help, the Lord is right there, where he's been all along, ready to give us what we truly need. And so often, his blessings and help come in the form of dear friends and family who act as the very hands of Jesus.

This is what it means to be a friend, to live in community. We're meant to support one another, love one another, care for one another, mutually. Ecclesiastes 4:9–10 tells us, "Two are better than one, because they have a good return for their labor: If either of them falls down, one can help the other up. But pity anyone who falls and has no one to help them up."

No one wants to be the one to fall down—but how blessed are we when we have dear friends to help us up again? Will we let them?

LOOKING INWARD: What makes you hesitant to ask for or receive help from a friend? What is the root of your need to feel and appear self-sufficient?

LOOKING UPWARD: Acknowledge to God that you can't do anything without his help, involvement, and care. Praise him for being strong when you are weak. Thank him for providing friends and family to come alongside you for support.

LOOKING OUTWARD: Practice receiving help. Even if you don't currently have a large-scale need or struggle, find a way to ask for and receive help this week, and next. Don't apologize, don't feel guilty—just say thank you.

Day 15

The Button Factory

Even after several months of some newfound, glorious extra sleep in our schedule, I couldn't shake an overwhelming sense of exhaustion. I'd be in a meeting or hurrying to finish a project and find myself daydreaming about driving five miles up the highway to a Holiday Inn Express just to hide and sleep. I'd hear a text or email ping, or watch someone approach me in the lobby of our school or church, and wish that I could just disappear.

Because I wasn't just exhausted, I was also hurt. And sad. And angry. Basically, I was a big ray of sunshine. This is what happens when you do everything for everyone for forever.

It's so easy to find yourself there. *Yes, I can edit that proposal. Yes, I can overhaul your website. Yes, I can plan the class party. Yes, I can host sixty college students for an after-church lunch.* Because technically I can—I'm available, I'm capable, and I have absolutely zero personal boundaries.

What's worse is I find myself doing things even when no one has asked. While this can be a good thing, sometimes repeatedly "helping" is less a support and more an enabling. When we're talking less about shoveling an elderly neighbor's driveway and more about continually filling the gap of a disorganized friend or a forever-behind coworker, it might be time to reevaluate.

All this running and working and doing and fixing and building and gap filling—it had left me in quite a state. *Don't people realize they're asking too much? Don't they see that I'm being worked into the ground? Don't they care that they're taking advantage?*

See how easily I can place the blame on everyone else?

One evening while I folded laundry (a task I always save for while the kids get ready for bed, because I'm a multitasking addict), I heard Breckin singing while he added toothpaste to his brush. I recognized it as the old camp song "My Name is Joe." I hadn't heard it in ages—you might remember it too. There are several versions, but the one from my childhood, and the one Breckin sang, goes something like this:

> Hi, my name is Joe
> And I work in a button factory.
> I've got a wife and two kids.
> One day my boss came to me and said
> Hey Joe, are you busy? I said no.
> He said turn this button with your right hand.

At this point you start cranking an invisible button with your right hand. The song repeats to add a button to turn with your left hand, then another to turn with your right foot, left foot, your head, however far you want to take it. By the final time through, you're cranking invisible buttons with everything you've got. Until the last two lines.

The boss asks one more time, "Hey Joe, are you busy?"

Joe, who's flailing in every direction trying to crank all these buttons, says, "I quit!"

As Breckin hit the final line, and I heard the words for the first time as an adult, I instinctively thought, *Joe is an idiot! I mean, your boss kept asking if you're busy. You kept saying no. You willingly took on an insane number of buttons. Instead of quitting, maybe you should have just said, "I'm busy" a long time ago. What a fool.*

And as soon as I finished mentally telling him off, Joe said, *You do the exact same thing.*

Quite a bit of sass for an imaginary factory worker, I thought. But he was right.

For some time, I had nurtured a growing resentment toward just about anyone who needed something from me. And my frustration didn't discriminate—it included both the poor soul who innocently requested my help on a project and the slackers who took advantage of my go-getter personality. It even included my own husband and children who might dare to ask if I knew where to find an extra roll of paper towels. I was angry that I had to do so much for so many people. I wanted to quit. Everything.

In fact, that phrase would slip out as I went about my day's tasks: "I quit everything."

When we reach this point, there are several questions we need to ask: *Why do I keep saying yes when I want to say no? Why am I overextending myself? What am I trying to prove and why do I think I have to do it all?*

Most of the time when we're drowning we're also, ironically, the ones holding the lifeline. But we're so busy trying to do everything and be everything that we can't pull ourselves to shore.

I get it: it can feel uncomfortable to decline a request for help. We don't want to hurt anyone's feelings or seem inept, and there are a lot of great causes out there—a lot of important projects, groups to support, and relationships to nurture. But we're not only harming ourselves when we take on too much. We're also bringing harm to our relationships and to those whom we set out to care for in the first place.

As we begin to feel run-down, our resentment grows. *How dare that class parent ask me to organize snacks for the valentine party? Does she think I have endless free time? Unbelievable that these church people keep expecting me to show up early to help just because I said I would. Don't they know I've had a long week? And the audacity of my family to assume I have the energy to wrestle shin guards, socks, and cleats onto my children's feet—it's just too much.*

And the resentment grows and grows.

But it doesn't have to be that way. We don't have to be that way.

We were never meant to do it all. God never intended for us to shoulder every burden or earn our worth. He created us with innate, unshakable value—we don't have to burn ourselves out trying to gain what we already have. And we can be comfortable with our own limitations. We need to rest in knowing that we—with our finite time, energy, and resources—are known and loved by a God who took on human limitations and walked this earth in rhythms of rest and work, self-care and care for others, being in the crowd and in solitude.

When someone asks for help on a new project or wants us to volunteer on our only quiet weekend, let's be honest about what we have left to give. Let's free ourselves to say, "Hey, I'd love to help, but I'm already turning all these other buttons. I can't take on another right now."

When we're not giving too much of ourselves, we can give joyfully. When we practice saying no, our yes has room to breathe.

LOOKING INWARD: Do you struggle to say no to requests of your time? What makes you nervous to disappoint people? Are you currently struggling with any bitterness or resentment over responsibilities you shouldn't have accepted?

LOOKING UPWARD: Invite the Lord into your schedule, your daily routine. Ask for help in discerning when to say yes, and when to say no. When to stretch yourself, and when to comfortably acknowledge your limitations.

LOOKING OUTWARD: Spend a few moments considering what it means to voice a brave, kind, firm no when needed. Craft and memorize your response.

Day 16

Cut Free

Let's get real here, friends. We need to address a common struggle among women: the exhausting and unbearable task of removing sweaty gym clothes after a good workout. Yes, I realize men sweat too—but it's not the same; their clothes are so loose and stretchy. Ours are tight, contoured, made to hold it all in. That's all fine and well until you're exhausted and the added layer of sweat adheres your top to your poor, fatigued body.

Recently at my gym, a few of us were lamenting this shared frustration after class when my friend Jill came around the corner and won the conversation by saying, "One time, I was so tired of trying to wrestle my sports bra off that I just grabbed the kitchen scissors and cut myself out." Jill is not a woman to be trifled with, friends. She is not messing around.

I was still giggling about this as I walked home. I was also a bit in awe. It was a bold move, and I admired it. I would wrestle and sweat and contort and curse my sports bra. I would never, ever consider just chopping the thing off.

In fact, I do this with more than just my gym clothes.

For one thing, I tend to engage in this on-again-off-again battle with cultural expectations. I hate feeling all this pressure—pressure to look a certain way, dress your children a certain way, act like this, decorate your house like that, travel here, work out there, DIY everything, get promoted, hire out help, eat this, never eat that, educate your children at home, at a public school, at a private school, at a Christian school, be Wonder Woman.

I resent needing to try to keep up with such a demanding lifestyle and appearance. It's just too much. The expectations are unending. I wrestle with them, fight them, and for a time may temper them. But for whatever reason, no matter how frustrating, I can't seem to bring myself to just cut them off. No matter how much I want to leave it all behind, I keep sweating through it. And while we may blame culture for perpetuating unrealistic and unhealthy expectations, we can only blame ourselves for choosing to abide by them.

The question is: Why do we wrestle with these pressures when we could simply refuse them? Why do we hold onto something that causes us so much strife? I wonder if there's a part of us, deep down, that is still searching for worth, looking to feel valued, and feeling plagued by the shame of our own imperfection. We can't make a clean break because we just aren't sure we've found true love, true acceptance, true security. But, dear friends, we have.

Paul writes in Ephesians 2 that *"because of his great love for us*, God, who is rich in mercy, made us alive with Christ even when we were dead in transgressions—it is by grace you have been saved" (4–5, emphasis mine). God so loved us, and so desired our love and friendship in return, that he created

a way for us to be reconciled to him. When we were at our worst, when we had nothing good to give, when we were life-less in our sin, he breathed into us new life—wide-awake life, vibrant life—because of his great love for us. It's not what we've done or what we do. It's all God's grace and God's gift to us, freely. We don't have to fit a mold, do anything, be any-thing. We are loved, valued, secure, period.

And we can cast off the shame. Our messes and mistakes have been forgiven. We've been cleansed. We have nothing to cover up, to hide. We've been made new, made clean. The messy house, growing stack of mail, or unkempt appearance should not threaten our hearts. They don't get to throw shade over us.

Still, it's hard to accept sometimes. I can't tell you how quickly my self-worth plummets if there's dust on the piano, dried drops of OJ on the counter, or a mess of receipts and gum wrappers in my bag. These seemingly trivial things leave me feeling like a failure. If I was on top of things, there would never be crumpled papers falling out of my purse and a pile of unfolded laundry at the end of my bed. All of my imperfec-tions, big and small, feed into this sense of shame—the sense that I'm not good enough, that I'll never be good enough.

So we wrestle and sweat and contort, trying to make sure everything is put together, our style is polished, our work is impressive, and our home is Instagrammable perfection. I'm not suggesting there's anything wrong with manicured nails, a clean house, and an organized purse—let's be honest, I love those things. The problem, though, is that we can exhaust and undermine our true selves trying to maintain an image because we feel that our worth depends on it.

But it doesn't. Our worth is set high, off the charts, determined by Jesus's great act of love. We can trust that we are loved wholly and valued fully, right now, as we are, when we look to the cross. We have nothing to earn—nothing to prove. We can cling to what we know is true and believe it with our whole hearts, even deep down where the fears and insecurities try to linger.

Sometimes, our greatest act of faith is ignoring the spilled dog food, the dust, and the pile of unfolded laundry. Sometimes, our greatest act of faith is ignoring our chipped nail polish and two-day-old ponytail. Because it's a hard no to the prevailing thought that our picturesque home and expert style determine our value.

We know who we are and to whom we belong. We know that we were fearfully and wonderfully made (Psalm 139:13–14), that God's love for us is deep, wide, vast, complete (Ephesians 3:17–18), and that he calls us his children (1 John 3:1). Our identity, value, and worth are not up for grabs.

A few dirty dishes in the sink don't make me a bad person—and they don't make you a bad person either. A bad hair day, or week, doesn't diminish your status as a daughter of the King. And your child's, ahem, *interesting* outfit doesn't mean anything other than you're kicking butt at raising an independent, creative child (go you!).

We don't have to hang on to these cultural expectations that are strangling us, draining us, running us ragged. We don't have to measure up to some arbitrary standard to earn love, acceptance, or worth—we already have it. If you've been trying and trying, wrestling and sweating, why not just cut yourself free?

LOOKING INWARD: What cultural expectations are strangling you? Why are you reluctant to completely let go of this pressure? Is there a part of you that doubts you're loved, valued, secure, as you are?

LOOKING UPWARD: Praise God for his unfailing love and unconditional acceptance. Invite him to help you learn to rest in it.

LOOKING OUTWARD: Stretch yourself this week. Choose one area to cut yourself free—make a choice to not be tyrannized by the state of your home, choose recreation over social climbing, be kind to the woman in the mirror. Be free.

Day 17

The Gift of a Kindred Spirit

One glance around the table and you'd have this group figured out. Dressed up, hair in place, bright smiles. Everyone's at ease, glasses are clinking, appetizers are arriving, and stories and laughter fill the table. *They look so happy. Everyone's having a good time. These people don't have a care in the world.*

Except they do. And I know this because this was us: Jon and I, plus two of our dearest couple-friends—Lauren and Jesse, Stell and Richard. (I can't even type their names without my heart swelling.)

One of the first things I noticed when I finished school was just how difficult it is to make friends out in "the real world." It's quite a shock to the system. You move from a campus setting where you're surrounded by instant community, into adulthood where you find yourself staring at another person in the grocery store thinking, "Do you want to be my friend? I see we both like coffee and tortilla chips."

Yet sometimes, magically—or rather, by the grace of God—you are gifted with kindred spirits. This was one of those times. And oh, we had such a great night. The food was incredible. The stories were unforgettable (my abs were sore the next day from laughing so hard). But this night was way more than just a good time—it was healing and restorative at a deep, deep level.

Each couple had arrived to the dinner with a burden. One had just watched an important business deal slip through their fingers. Another had received news that a longtime friend had passed away. And Jon and I were in the thick of trying to kick-start a new life while still living under the painful side effects of the old one.

We shared the tough stuff, but we also shared the good stuff. Our time together wasn't morose, but it wasn't fluff either. We all need those people in our lives—the ones with whom you can laugh hard, cry openly, or sit in silence. We need those people who don't expect us to be super awesome, or proper, or *on*. We need those people who aren't going to flee when they see us at our worst, because they know we're human and don't expect us to be perfect.

It's not just the fun times that are better together—even the painful is richer when we walk together. After all, great company triumphs over great pain and great loss. This is why we go to be with people in the hospital or at a funeral. And this is equally true in the less dramatic day-to-day moments. It's why our hearts feel lifted after a few quick email exchanges with a long-distance kindred spirit. It's why a merry, lively evening out with friends can be so nourishing for the soul.

When Jesus went to Gethsemane, he knew he would soon be betrayed by a friend, arrested, mocked, crucified, and separated from his father. The Son of God did not simply

motor through, keeping his feelings close to his chest. He didn't pretend everything was fine, or hide out alone. When he was truly filled with sorrow, "to the point of death," he chose a couple friends to sit by his side (Matthew 26:36–38).

This isn't about being a part of the in-crowd or being popular. And this isn't about becoming an extrovert and surrounding yourself with hundreds of besties. It's about mutual support. It's about knowing and being known. It's about enjoying the gift of a kindred spirit.

Somehow, though, we tend to drift into isolation. I get it—maintaining friendships requires time, and we tend to reserve that time for productivity. Can we really put our schedules on pause in order to just enjoy the company of a friend? I think we have to. Nurturing our souls isn't a solo task. We were created for community, and we're at our best when we can care and be cared for, celebrate and be celebrated, love and be loved. Hold your friends close, and revel in the gift of a kindred heart.

There is a beauty and wholeness that shines through true friendships, highlighting all of our hopes and dreams for our world. We're reminded of the good, of what's to come, of our promised future—a world healed and whole, a world in perfect harmony. This is why we're drawn to others, and this is why we long for close relationships. It's a taste of heaven—an imperfect version, yet still so sweet.

We're growing stronger, wiser, and more gracious together. We're taking on life together and laughing until our sides hurt. We may be fighting different battles, but our arms are tightly linked. We're celebrating big things and little things. When a deal finally comes through, we gather to celebrate. When we bravely take on a risk with a new project, a new relationship, or a new haircut, we cheer each other on—we are one another's biggest fans. And when the doctor calls with a hard diagnosis, or when a battle rages with one of our children, we cry right alongside each other, and bring love in the form of coffee, meals, and prayers.

Because together, the good things are better. Because together, the heavy things are lighter. And there is a sweetness to even the little things when we know we're not alone.

LOOKING INWARD: Who are your soul friends? What value do they add to your life? What do you desire most in these types of relationships? What dynamics might be keeping you from enjoying close friendships?

LOOKING UPWARD: Praise God for the community he has brought into your life and the way he works through it to love, bless, and care for you. If you do not have this type of community, praise God for his personal love and care, and ask for his provision in bringing friendships of mutual love and support.

LOOKING OUTWARD: Spend a few moments reflecting on some of the sweet relationships in your life. Write a note or two (text or email works!) to express your gratitude for the friendship.

Day 18

Drowning Puppies

At twenty-one I headed to seminary—energetic, bubbly, excited. My undergraduate experience had done well in shaping in me a worldview that said, "Hey! All of this matters! Everything on this earth is connected to God and our faith!" This fueled me. This is why I packed up my belongings in the back of a Saturn station wagon, drove to Boston's North Shore, and arrived on campus, sight unseen.

People were confused. Why was a seemingly normal, nice, upbeat young lady going to seminary? Isn't that reserved for serious older men? "So you want to preach?" they'd say, faces scrunched.

This took me aback—no, I did not want to preach. But not for the reasons they were thinking. I simply didn't want to stand on a stage. I didn't even want to visualize myself on a stage. What I wanted to do was inspire people to broaden their view of faith—to engage the world with an energy and belief that all of this matters to God, that he's working in and healing it all.

When preaching courses were offered, as they tend to be at seminaries, I steered clear and opted for courses like

theodicy or ancient Greek. Anything that kept me from standing in front of people.

So naturally, a couple years ago when my pastor and good friend, Jared, asked if I would preach at our church, I said sure. (And then spent the day-of in a café down the street stress-texting my sister while fighting to keep my stomach from emptying itself.)

But guess what? I survived.

And after a few times my legs weren't shaking anymore. I think I even managed to make one almost-natural hand gesture. And over time, I discovered the ideal heel-height for retaining femininity in a male-dominated world while not risking an embarrassing fall. As it turns out, preaching is a great way to get your message out and inspire people. Who knew?

Years of listening to Jared's sermons had proven to be a natural training ground, but I still worried that bypassing those seminary courses may have been a mistake. Which is why I jumped at his invitation to join a preaching group. We meet once a month or so to discuss books and critique one another's sermons. Not only am I the only one with no real preaching training, but I am also the only female. So I fit in really well.

Still, it's been a great experience. Even simply listening in on sermon critique has proven invaluable. Over time, I've come to know each member's particular bent. Jim is going to highlight the existence or nonexistence of signposts and a consistent message. As a musician-turned-pastor, Scott will instinctively evaluate the delivery for tone and cadence. And John will always be the voice for shortening, editing down—less is more.

At our most recent gathering, we were focused in on John's angle, looking at a sermon that had gone long, included too many nuggets. Paul chimed in, speaking to the difficulty of keeping a message concise when your research has unearthed so many interesting and important pieces. "It's hard, because it's all good stuff. No one wants to edit out good stuff," he said, "but you have to drown some puppies."

As a big fan of little furry animals, this phrase stuck with me. Especially because I had a sneaking suspicion that I had some editing to do in other areas of my life.

All these years after seminary the words energetic, bubbly, and excited no longer fit. I had the same desires, the same dreams, same message, but I was so tired. I desperately needed rest—and after years of saying, "next month will be quiet," I was beginning to realize that "next month" never came. It wasn't the holidays, or the end of the school year, or the way everything kicks off all at once in the fall—it was me.

I know I'm not alone here. Even after clearing some commitments and making a practice of saying no, we're often surprised to find ourselves overbooked. Yet we do it to ourselves. We'll receive an invitation to dinner, scan our calendar for any remaining holes, and then add a reservation to our only free day that month. As fun projects, groups, or activities enter our radar we think, "Sounds great!" and in a flash the dates and to-dos are added to our phones.

It doesn't take long before our calendars overwhelm us and we're left wondering what happened to that quiet month we'd imagined.

The morning after our preaching group met I filled my largest mug with coffee and flipped open my computer—anxiety

rising as I remembered all the undealt-with emails, asks, and invitations waiting just a click away. I began scanning through the emails—new dates for a prayer group, an invitation to an art exhibit, a request to volunteer in my children's school, an upcoming book club. All good things. All things that I immediately wanted to RSVP to with a resounding "Yes! I'm in!"

Yet something inside gave me pause—my tired, run-down, almost extinguished self. The part of me that was buried somewhere deep inside of the productivity machine known as Jen Wise. I knew what I had to do. It was time to drown some puppies.

We'll find that we'll often have to decline and delete some good things, things we want to do or be a part of, in order to have what we want most—a healthy, full, real life. A life with energy, because it's a life that offers rest.

But it's so hard, right? We don't like missing out on something fun or meaningful in the name of a healthy pace. Things like family gatherings, dinner invitations, and opportunities to connect with friends are hard to pass up simply to slow down. It feels really uncomfortable to say, "I'm too busy for this prayer group." I mean, prayer is good! What kind of monster bails on a prayer group? But not every good thing arrives with good timing. Not every good thing is good for us, right now.

My son Breckin loves tomatoes with all his heart. He will eat baskets upon baskets of tomatoes, and wash it down with a V8. So nutritious! So much goodness! Yet at some point it's not so good—it's just too much. All those vitamins don't seem so great when you're curled up in bed with a stomachache.

The life we want—a healthy, full, vibrant life—requires continuous discipline with our calendars and commitments,

even when it comes to things we enjoy. The book club may expand our relationships and our minds, the volunteer opportunity may move a valued initiative forward, and our relatives might be thrilled to have us join that picnic. But all this goodness doesn't seem so great anymore when we're riddled with anxiety and making ourselves sick.

This isn't the life that God imagines for us. This isn't the way we're called to live. God's way brings health, wholeness, and peace, three things we so desperately crave. Somehow though we fool ourselves into thinking that we know best. That more is better. That our success and happiness will bloom when we seize every opportunity that comes our way—take everything we can get. But all that great stuff begins to choke out the very life we're trying to create.

Proverbs 15 reminds us that we form our lives by the choices we make. Eugene Peterson paraphrases it this way in verse 32: "An undisciplined, self-willed life is puny; an obedient, God-willed life is spacious" (MSG).

Is your life spacious? Or is it so crammed full of good things that it's closing in on you?

When we follow God's way—the way of rest and Sabbath and trusting in him—more than just our calendar opens up. We'll find we can relax, breathe deeply, be free to enjoy the people who have been given to us, notice the beauty in the everyday, hear God's voice. We can stretch out, spin, see the sun again.

A spacious life says no to our natural inclination to grasp every good thing within reach, and a resounding yes to the greater good—a life that is vibrant, energized, and at peace. A spacious life means we know God's desire for us is so good.

And that we can follow his rhythms of grace into the life we really want.

LOOKING INWARD: Do you ever feel like all the good opportunities—groups, projects, activities—are closing in on you? What drives your desire to grasp all of these things? What are you afraid will happen if you decide to let some go?

LOOKING UPWARD: Thank God for his goodness—his desire to see us energized, healthy, and free. Praise him for his faithfulness to continue to call, lead, and woo us into the wide open spaces he envisions for us.

LOOKING OUTWARD: Look over your calendar for the past few months, and the month to come. Where do you feel that your schedule is suffocating you? What good things should you release in order to receive the greater good—a life at peace, vibrant with energy, trusting that God is in control?

Day 19

Provision

It was time to exhale. Jon's new company was a year old. We had survived the short-term transition from one career to the next, from unknown to, well, as known as a start-up can be. Jon had a steady stream of clients. His team had grown nicely into their roles. Paychecks were being given out. This may sound basic, but these basics are enormous when you're in your early years of a business. It wasn't time to slough off or take a two-month vacation to Europe, but it was time to relax a little, loosen our grip from the roller coaster we'd been on.

And we did—in spurts and stops. We'd revel in having weekends off with the kids, in how much more sleep we were getting, in how much better we felt getting to the gym consistently. But then something would come into focus—a contract that still sat unsigned, a client who was wavering on a project, a random week four months out that was unsettlingly unscheduled, unneeded, and therefore unpaying. And that grip would tighten right back up. There would be no exhale.

In a way, it felt silly. We were so thankful for the ease of this transition. We were acutely aware of God's hand in our

soft landing, in his provision. Yet as grateful as we were to God for these gifts, we found ourselves fearful that he would take them away. It didn't matter that we'd experienced his faithfulness, that we knew he was good. Deep down we still felt the burden to shore things up on our own. It seemed safer that way. After all, everything had fallen to pieces before— shouldn't we do everything we could to prevent it from happening again?

We all struggle with this from time to time, don't we? We think God isn't who we've known him to be, or that just when we begin to trust him he'll change his mind about us. Maybe he doesn't really care. Maybe he's run out of patience. Maybe he used to want good for us, but now he's indifferent. Maybe we'd better learn to take care of ourselves.

Yet the Bible is clear that God is the same yesterday, today, and forever. James 1:17 tells us that God "does not change like shifting shadows." If he loved you yesterday, he loves you today. If he was with you in the valley, he'll be with you on the plains or the mountaintop. If he's provided in the past, you can look ahead without fear—his generosity doesn't run out. In fact, that very same verse reminds us that every good and perfect gift comes from his hand.

But we don't particularly like to be on the receiving end of generosity, do we? That feels weak, needy. We like to feel strong, independent. We live in a culture where we take pride in earning what we have or at least deserving what we have. If we have a lot, that means we're successful, admirable, popular, maybe even good-looking. We've made it. It's a very different posture that views everything we have as a gift from a good God.

When we respond to God's giving, we stop trying to grab and attain and stockpile. When we respond to God's giving, we know that no matter how much we want to protect ourselves, it is God, in his consistent goodness, who will provide. When we respond to God's giving, we acknowledge that he is all-powerful—and we are not. He holds the world in his hands—we don't.

Maybe that was the tension Jon and I were feeling. When we looked back, we could see God's hand—yet we'd made so much progress, we really felt that we shouldn't need his hand anymore. We were back up on our feet, and we wanted to be back to handling our own problems, holding our own, building our future. *Thanks for getting us up and running again, God. We'll take it from here.* But that sort of thinking, as we had already discovered, only leads to anxiety.

Maybe it's not just in the hardest times of life that we have to release control to God. And maybe it's not just a big one-time decision when everything has gone haywire. Maybe it's a choice we need to make every single day. Maybe it's a choice that's just as important, and maybe even more difficult, to make when life feels even, smooth.

Let's choose to let God take the lead. Let's let go of our obsession with getting, so we can gratefully receive what he has in store for us. We don't need to get so stressed about what may or may not happen tomorrow, or next month, or half a year from now. God will still be here, still all-powerful, still all-loving, still God.

LOOKING INWARD: Do you find it more difficult to cling to God and rely on him when life is going your way? Why?

LOOKING UPWARD: Praise God for his generous provision. Open your hands to him, palms to the sky, and name the ways he has provided for you, offering your thanks.

LOOKING OUTWARD: Make a practice of being less occupied with getting by responding to God's giving. This week, when you notice yourself worried about getting more, getting better—or being more, being better—take a moment, open your hands to the sky, and thank God for his good gifts.

Day 20

No Space

The universe shifted several years ago when my dad got his first iPhone. With four kids and group chat, the possibilities were endless. My dad is active, relational, creative, curious, and funny—and the myriad group texts that have ensued since his entry into the world of iMessage prove just that. Selfies of him eating Twizzlers while off-roading in his Jeep. Continual texts that are his version of live-tweeting an all-day garden project. A video series of my mom eating Skinny Cow ice cream (don't try to make sense of it). It's all very weird, and I absolutely love it.

Several times a year, we'll all get an urgent update to go outside in the middle of the night because some sort of lunar or celestial event is taking place. As long as the event isn't taking place at three in the morning, I'll usually set a reminder on my phone and try to see what all the fuss is about. I say *try* because other than one time, when we had the good fortune of being on a road trip during an eclipse, I have not been able to see a single one of these shooting stars, blood moons, or comets. I'll slip on my sandals and a

hoodie, run outside, and remember that oh, right, my view is completely blocked here.

My parents live in a quiet neighborhood with ample space. Their home sits back off the road surrounded by a large yard, a sprinkling of tall, leafy trees, and gardens. Behind their house it's a natural tangle of sumac trees, raspberry bushes, and deer paths. By contrast, we live in the first rung of historic neighborhoods outside of Philadelphia. It's tight and chaotic. There are eighteen homes on our block that take up the same amount of space as my parents have in their yard. Our street is one lane and a dead end—you literally drive in and back out (I bet you didn't know those exist). We are the only house with a yard (and I use that term loosely, since it's likely the size of your kitchen). Street lights beam in at night and the sounds and smells of restaurants and businesses waft through our windows. Our house is perfect for knowing your neighbors, walkability, and late-night takeout. It's not as great for privacy, quiet, and seeing stars.

When we step outside to capture one of these once-a-decade type events, there are too many buildings, too many lights. I'll walk up and down the street, trying different angles. I'll turn in circles, cross to the other sidewalk, hop up on someone's stoop. But it's an unnaturally bright and starless sky, and it's a very rare occasion to find the moon at all from our little spot on the earth. It's just too crowded, too congested.

I often feel this in my daily life. When we head to Traverse City for the summer, it's not just the physical space that feels good, but the mental space that promises a rebirth of sorts. Sure, we may have work, our kids may have some camps or
</>

activities, but compared to life at home, it is smooth sailing. When work is done, when the boys have been picked up from camp, there is little else to worry about besides what to throw on the grill and if we feel like hitting the beach for a sunset swim.

The problem is that usually we make our way through the calendar year with little-to-no mental space. It's not just that we have too much on our plate, but that we're quick to fill up any space that's left. Need to wait two minutes for the microwave? Click on your phone and check the news. Stuck in a slow-moving line? Pound through some of those emails. Walking from the living room to the kitchen? May as well browse Facebook for thirty seconds. And as we fill our minds with more and more noise, we simultaneously whine and complain, wondering where God is. *Why isn't he more clear? Where is his voice, his direction?*

But God answers us when we call—he is there when we're in need (Psalm 91:15). It's not that God has disappeared or that he's ignoring us. He's here, he's involved, acting, speaking—but we can't hear his voice or see his movement because we're inundated with noise, clouded by a million voices, numbed by distractions.

God speaks to us through Scripture, through his brilliant creation, through his people, and straight to our heart through his Spirit. But do we notice? Do we take time to not only read, but also sit with Scripture—to allow it to sink into our minds and souls, to be still and listen, to respond? Do we experience God revealing himself to us through powerful waves at the shore, bright pink blooms in spring, or tiny little bird legs on our windowsill? Do we have any room left within us to notice him stirring our hearts?

I think most of us want to hear God's voice. We want to find peace and direction and answers and love. Yet we seek comfort in all these other voices.

I'm no different. As Jon and I navigated the on-ramping of a new life, a new business, new routines, new everything—while simultaneously letting go of the old routines, old stress, old habits—it was overwhelming at times. I'd come home from running errands, park my car, and then open my Facebook app and just scroll through the lives of hundreds of online friends. I'd read articles about anything that caught my eye, and skim silly BuzzFeed lists and the like. Waste of time? Of course. But in some way, I subconsciously could not make myself reenter the world. I had this sense that if I stayed there in my car, very quiet and very still, the world wouldn't notice me—I'd be safe inside the nonworld of the internet, slipping into an easy forgetting of reality.

The thing is, while zoning out on Facebook may have kept me from having to deal with my real, actual life, it was only temporary. When I looked up from my phone and opened the car door, all the same responsibilities, problems, and stress were there waiting for me.

And beyond that, while we search for comfort and peace, rounding up voices to distract us, all we're really doing is blocking the voice of the only One who truly offers those things to us. When our minds are flooded with photos of one thousand friends, updates from our favorite brands, celebrity advice, and breaking news, there's no space left. We can spin around and try different angles, but we've effectively drowned out the one true voice in a sea of noise.

Can we clear away some of the noise? I'm not saying we need to ditch our smartphones, quit social media, and take a vow of silence. But could we slow down, quiet down? What if we set guidelines around how often and when we browse Facebook and Instagram? What if we make a habit of turning our phone to silent in the evenings? Or refuse to check our email until we've taken a moment to pray, be still, listen, receive? What if, when our thumb instinctively reaches for an app, we used that as a trigger to click the phone off and offer up a prayer?

A few weeks ago, our family spent a long weekend at the shore with friends. We rented a huge beach house to share, loaded in an inordinate amount of groceries and supplies, and settled in for a weekend of lazy days and long nights. That first evening after all the kids were in bed, we sat out on the sprawling porch. I glanced out to the quiet night sky and was completely caught off guard—stars. Stars! "Oh my goodness! There are stars! I forgot stars exist!" I said.

Once we allow ourselves to clear some mental clutter, we'll be surprised to hear God's voice—to realize that he's been here all along, moving in us, working on our behalf, speaking to us, calling us, offering peace. We only need to dim the noise and we're in for a beautiful display.

LOOKING INWARD: Do you find yourself filling any extra space with noise? What do you gravitate to—social media, Netflix, the news? Why do you do this, and what benefits might you gain if you cleared some of the mental clutter?

LOOKING UPWARD: Sit quietly before the Lord. Invite him to speak, move—and wait without expectation. Practice being comfortable with the calm.

LOOKING OUTWARD: What will you do this week to clear some of the mental noise? Write down your commitment and stick to it.

Day 21

Two Pockets

It was one of those days. Okay, it was more than a day—let's say a series of days. I was still grateful, deep down, for answers to Jon's health woes. Grateful, deep down, for a way forward. But at times it felt really deep down and covered over by frustration, exhaustion, and the reality of how unfair this still felt. I'd dip into depression, and I'd come up for air. I'd dip again.

But then there would be a string of funny texts from a friend, a lovely dinner party, a chat on the sidewalk with a neighbor. Or a coffee meet-up where we both laughed and cried, a night out on the town, a brunch that lingered past noon. It was through these things that God gave me relief. It was through these people, these sweet friends, these little walking lightbearers, that my soul was lightened, my head lifted, and my heart made full.

Because love is healing, and love puts things right. Love restores us. Love makes us whole.

And this is the good news of the gospel: the power of perfect love.

"This is how much God loved the world: He gave his Son, his one and only Son. And this is why: so that no one need be destroyed; by believing in him, anyone can have a whole and lasting life. God didn't go to all the trouble of sending his Son merely to point an accusing finger, telling the world how bad it was. He came to help, to put the world right again" (John 3:16–17 MSG).

Because of Christ's love, we are offered new life. Because of his love, we are made healed and whole. Because of his love, we are promised that our world will be made right again.

It's for this reason that we have hope even in the midst of struggles, broken relationships, and pain. This is no pie-in-the-sky, self-medicating religion. This is faith that fully sees and mourns the brokenness of this world, all the while brimming with hope for our promised future of restoration. And guess what? This promise is already working itself out, here and now.

Right now the world rages and wars, and right now God is moving through families and friendships, healing hearts and restoring communities. Right now the sick ache in their beds, and right now God's comfort swells and surrounds. Right now creation bends and breaks, and right now God receives praises from the grasses and the seas.

We are a people who live in the tension between the bad and the good, today's sorrow and a future hope. We don't need to be naïve to the pain and suffering around us, but neither do we need to drown in a sea of despair. When we understand God's unfolding plan, our hearts can be a place where both sorrow and joy live in harmony. I love how the mystic Parker Palmer describes this dynamic: "We need a coat with two pockets. In one pocket there is dust, and in the other pocket

there is gold. We need a coat with two pockets to remind us who we are."[4]

We are people who are both broken and restored. We are people who experience both hardship and hope. We are people who see the fragmentation of our world, and the healing hand of God amidst it all. We are a people with two pockets—dust and gold.

There's no question that this world, and our lives, are marred by the sin of this world. We'll get sick. We'll be hurt by a friend. We'll experience rejection. Some dreams will be dashed. We'll deal with unemployment, infertility, loneliness. Conflict will plague our relationships. But while we may get knocked down from time to time, we're continually made new by perfect love. And we're called to shine forth the gold in a land of dust.

Maybe it's okay to mourn and praise. Maybe it's okay to acknowledge the hurts, the disappointments, even while thanking God for his goodness. Maybe it's okay to feel broken from this world and yet simultaneously renewed through God's love. This is what his love does, and we are invited to pass it on.

First John 4:11–12 implores us to do just this. "Dear friends, since God so loved us, we also ought to love one another. No one has ever seen God; but if we love one another, God lives in us and his love is made complete in us." Our friends and neighbors don't need a reminder of the dust—it's been kicked up. Clouds surround. What they need is the promise of the gold. And the greatest way to pass on God's love is by letting it flow through us.

As we walk through our days and weeks, may we hold strong to the promise that our world will one day be healed

and whole. May we not turn a blind eye to brokenness, but walk confidently, knowing that even amidst the dust there is gold. Let's carry armfuls of love like a giant bouquet, and let's pass it out generously as we look forward with hope and expectation to the day our world is made right again.

LOOKING INWARD: Do you live with a balanced understanding of the brokenness of this world, and the hope of Christ? Or does your focus and demeanor lean one way—toward dust—or toward gold? Why?

LOOKING UPWARD: Open your heart to the God who loves us, and share both your worries and your hope, your sorrow and your praises. Thank him for being a God who reigns through it all and works in it all. Thank him that while this world is still broken, we can see that he is here, working and moving— he never leaves us.

LOOKING OUTWARD: Collect some sand or dirt in a small jar—it's completely acceptable to pull something out of the recycling bin. Then add in a gold-colored trinket or a spray-painted rock, or maybe just sprinkle in some glitter. Set this jar on a windowsill or anywhere else you'll see it during the day, and allow it to be a reminder that while we're broken, we're being made new—while we face struggle and trial, God's love is already at work making all things new.

Day 22

Perfecting the Playlist

This past summer, I organized an outdoor movie series in a park a few blocks from our house. Working with Meade, a friend and pastor at our church, we quickly pulled together dates, chose films, and were on our way to outdoor movie bliss. With a simple website and a Facebook page, we began to share the events with our local friends. It took off. Within a week, word had spread like wildfire and our plan—which was set to accommodate a few hundred people—needed to be redone.

We ordered a gigantic inflatable movie screen and gazillions of glow sticks, made bigger signs to hang, and purchased inordinate amounts of popcorn kernels. (This still proved to not be enough, as Meade's wife, Amy, spent the entire first night scavenging every grocery store in driving distance for additional popcorn.)

Details were important before, but with so many people, the pressure was on to get it right. Nothing to fear—I am a details person, especially for any kind of party or gathering. I genuinely care how the lights are hung, what the food looks

like, and if everything matches. And so when it came time to build a pre-movie playlist for the night, I didn't just scan Spotify for my favorite songs. I meticulously crafted what, in my opinion, was a masterpiece.

I have a whole system for building a playlist, and I'll share the steps so you too can create a masterpiece for your next event. Start by bopping around your favorite albums, artists, and playlists. As you do so, think through the event. Who is the audience? What mood are you hoping to create? What level of energy do you want to interject? Will the listeners be talking, dancing, mingling, waiting, having fun? What are your highest values here—what defines your playlist?

Once you've answered these questions, start adding songs. Snag some favorites, explore for new ones, and include a few unexpected picks. Next, if this isn't a "shuffle all" situation, make sure the song order flows and is balanced. But wait— you're not done. The final and most important step remains: edit mercilessly. Mercilessly. Listen through the list start to finish and delete anything that doesn't match 100 percent. Wrong audience? Deleted. Too much energy, not enough? Deleted. Your favorite song ever, but the vibe is off? Deleted.

Go back the next day and edit again. If any song doesn't meet your highest values, it's gone.

We welcomed around a thousand guests to our first movie night. As we popped popcorn and handed out glow sticks, the songs looped through. Families set up blankets; friends shared picnics; kids ran, laughed, danced. It was perfect. There were three hours between the first arrivers and show time, but that playlist kept the atmosphere happy, fun, exciting, special, and positive. Song after song, the feeling held.

Editing down a perfect playlist takes significantly more time than simply throwing together your favorite tunes. But music sets a mood. It's incredibly powerful to create the feel and vibe, to draw out the emotions you want associated with that night—especially when you align everything with a common goal.

While this concept has always seemed obvious to me in matters of party music, sadly it's taken time to infiltrate the rest of my life. I haven't always been so good at editing down or aligning my life around a goal. I'm not sure I could have even defined what my highest goals and values were. Sure, I could give you the general answers of loving God, following Jesus, close relationships, and healthy living. And yes, these are overarching guiding principles—the strongest ones, I hope. Yet, underneath those broad umbrellas, to what was I aligning my choices? What criteria was I measuring against?

Most of us care about a lot of things. We care about healthy relationships. We care about the needy in our cities and around the world. We care about developing a nurturing home. We care about our careers, about professional growth, about gaining influence. We care about our families—about raising kind, smart, brave children. We care about the earth, about art, about financial security, about nutritious food, about resilience, faith, hard work, social status, politics, education, and community health.

There are so many things to value—some more and less noble. It's no wonder that we get bogged down, overbook ourselves, and feel pulled in a hundred directions. How do we know what to do and what to leave undone? How do we know when to step up and when to step back? How can we put off something we care about?

As I began to seek more downtime, less busyness, more breathing room, I felt caught. So much of what I was doing was because it mattered to me. So much of what filled my days and weeks were activities and projects that were good— for me, for my family, for neighbors, my church, the world. But I knew I couldn't go on this way—scattered, exhausted. While I was giving a lot to many things I cared about, that meant I couldn't give much to the things I cared about most.

It was time to do some merciless editing. But first, I needed some criteria: What were my top goals? What were my highest values? As I began to brainstorm, it was too broad. As Jon will attest to, I care a lot about a lot of things. Apparently, it can be exhausting for other people, or so I've heard. With honest reflection, I knew it was exhausting for me too. I had to keep editing.

I found the inspiration I needed in one of my favorite books, *The Inner Voice of Love* by Henri Nouwen. In it he shares, "Exhaustion, burnout, and depression are not signs that you are doing God's will. God is gentle and loving. God desires to give you a deep sense of safety in God's love. Once you have allowed yourself to experience that love fully, you will be better able to discern who you are being sent to in God's name."[5]

Exhaustion, burnout, and depression were all too familiar. I knew this wasn't the way of Jesus. Yes, God cares about the whole world, every broken piece, every single person. Still, he hasn't called me to carry the world or heal everything that's broken. He hasn't sent me to every people group. If I wanted to drop the burden I was never intended to carry, I needed to submerse myself in his love—knowing it had power to

hold the world, heal the world, and reach every single person. Knowing his love for me is complete and secure, period. Knowing that he has prepared me to share that very love (Ephesians 2:4–10). I've been sent.

It wasn't fast. Deep work takes time. I prayed. I meditated. I journaled. I prayed more. I talked to Jon. And in the end, I landed on three main ways I felt sent—three core values: raising children who know in their bones that they are loved and valuable, ministering to and shepherding my local community, and sharing my voice through writing and speaking.

While it required time and intentionality, defining my core values made editing my calendar and commitments infinitely simpler. As requests came in to help with a project, take on new work, or join a group, I could quickly evaluate if it was right for me. It also removed the guilt—it's not that I didn't care, it's that I needed to pour my time and energy into what I cared about most, into whom I was being sent.

Sure, there will be and should be some things we do just for fun, enjoyment, and relaxation. And there will be times we step out of the box because we have some wiggle room and want to help someone out. But we only have space for those things when we scrupulously edit our commitments.

That new activity doesn't fit? That weekly group doesn't align with your values? It's playing a different tune than the one you're singing? Deleted.

LOOKING INWARD: What are your core values—to whom have you been sent? What are the things only you can do—the things you can do best and you care about most? Reflect, pray, brainstorm, whittle down, until you have something concise.

LOOKING UPWARD: Invite God into the process of determining where your time, talents, and energy are best given. Rest in his love that will carry what you need to set down. Commit to following, loving, and worshiping him as the highest value—the umbrella over all else.

LOOKING OUTWARD: Write your core values at the top of a sheet of paper. Then, underneath, make a list of your current and upcoming commitments, as well as any options before you. Go back through your list and highlight everything that aligns with your core values. Look over what's left—what needs to be deleted? Don't be afraid to edit mercilessly. As new opportunities come your way, evaluate each by your core values.

Day 23

Unexpected Creations

There is little worse than the combination of raging hunger and an empty fridge. I find myself in this predicament about once a month. I really do try to stay on top of grocery shopping. Jon did the grocery shopping for years, but now it's bounced back to my side of the column. It fits with my love for cooking and menu planning just fine, so as far as household responsibilities go, I don't mind it. But our kids eat everything in sight. And there are some weeks that just get away from me. That is how I found myself staring into our bare refrigerator, panic rising.

No leftovers. No avocados (which can sub for a whole meal, in my opinion). No eggs. Nothing.

All I could rustle up was the tail end of a carton of Chobani, a dried-out lemon half, and some stray browning strawberries. This would have to be it. I spread the yogurt in the bottom of a shallow bowl and slivered the strawberries so they'd cover more ground. The dried-out lemon offered no juice, but it could be zested. So lemon zest, a dash of cinnamon, a drizzle of maple syrup, and the crumbs from a bag of pistachios topped it all off.

I set the bowl down on the table next to my computer. Wow. It was beautiful. I snapped a photo for Instagram and dug in. Every bite was perfection—bits of strawberry, a good tart edge from the zest, a salty crunch from the pistachio crumbs. It killed me there was no one home to give it a try, to share in my delight.

I've made a bowl of yogurt for myself many times. Many, many times. And I've thrown fruit on top, or mixed in peanut butter. It's all been decent. But it wasn't until my fridge was bare that the absolute perfect parfait presented itself. It came at just the right time.

I had begun to run out of energy and needed a boost—even if it was in the form of a happy little meal. Physical recovery is really hard work. And recovering our lives was really hard work. I was tired of adjusting to new footing, making tough decisions, stepping out of my comfort zone, and challenging my assumptions. Every couple months, part of me begged, "Isn't this enough? We've made progress, we've changed. Can we be done here?"

How much more could be stripped away, remade, replaced? We had so little left to give. It was then, that these words in Isaiah spoke to my soul: "Do you not know? Have you not heard? The Lord is the everlasting God, the Creator of the ends of the earth. He will not grow tired or weary, and his understanding no one can fathom. He gives strength to the weary and increases the power of the weak. Even youths grow tired and weary, and young men stumble and fall; but those who hope in the Lord will renew their strength. They will soar on wings like eagles; they will run and not grow weary, they will walk and not be faint" (Isaiah 40:28–31).

Strength to the weary? Power for the weak? Yes, please. I'll take it all.

Here we were, on this journey of learning to trust in God's promises, rest in his care, and let him do the heavy lifting. And when we began to tire of the process, the answer, again and always, was to hope in him.

We don't need to fear the stripping away, because while it may not be fun and we may feel worn down at times, we have the protection and love of a God who never grows weary or tired. He never wears out on shepherding us, guiding us, healing us, refilling us. Sometimes it's when everything is stripped away, when we feel we have nothing left, that God takes what's left—the bits and pieces we may think are unimportant or unimpressive—and makes the most stunning, unexpected, new creation. If we'll place our hope in him, he will renew our strength, make us new, give us fresh energy for this beautiful life he's putting together for us, with us.

Are you empty? Worn out? Weary?

Maybe you've been recovering from addiction—and eight months in, you're tired of the daily fight. Maybe you've been walking faithfully, trusting God will see your family through in a season of unemployment—and while God has been faithful so far, you're worn out on the waiting. Or maybe you've been choosing kindness and love with a difficult family member—and after a decade of unreturned grace you're not sure how much more you want to extend.

If this is you, allow your heart to echo the psalmist, as you cry out to God. "Hear my cry, O God; listen to my prayer. From the ends of the earth I call to you, I call as my heart grows faint; lead me to the rock that is higher than I. For you

have been my refuge, a strong tower against the foe. I long to dwell in your tent forever and take refuge in the shelter of your wings" (Psalm 61:1–4).

Let's cry out to God when we're fading, when we've had enough. When we don't know how to keep moving forward, he'll carry us. He'll offer us shelter. He'll renew our energy. And when we feel we've given all we've got, that we have so little left, let's take heart—because God has saved exactly what he needs, the perfect pieces to make something unexpected, beautiful, new. You can count on it.

LOOKING INWARD: Is there a part of you that feels run-down or weary? What is wearing you out?

LOOKING UPWARD: Praise our God, our shelter, our refuge, our strong tower against the foe. Our God never grows weary, never tires of caring for us or for this world—thank him for it. Ask him for fresh energy—to fly on wings like eagles. Put your hope in him, and trust that he will renew your strength.

LOOKING OUTWARD: Allow yourself to dream. Don't be afraid to get excited about what God is up to in your life. We may not know the future, but we know he holds it, and we know he is good. Imagine a few scenarios—as wild or tame as you like—and offer them up to God, praising him for the good work he is doing in your life.

Day 24

Warning Signs

One morning I poured a protein shake into my purse. I'd been up early—already hit the gym, showered, folded laundry, dried my hair. I was running downstairs to make breakfast for the boys, get the cooler packed for our lunch between activities, and get us out the door. Our schedule was full, my mind was full, my hands were full. But I was feeling pretty good—after all, the sun was barely up and I'd already had a pretty productive day. Yet as I attempted to drop a sweater into my bag, I watched, in confusion and disbelief, as I instead turned my glass over and poured out the rest of my shake. I saw it happening and couldn't even stop myself.

This is always the way when I've taken on too much, tangibly or mentally. Pouring a shake into my bag is just a start. I've driven off from a gas station with the hose still attached to my car. I hop out of my car without putting it in park and turning it off (this is how I repeatedly drove into the building at my seminary that housed our mailroom). I mess up dates—wrong months, wrong years—and you might notice that I'm swapping out words and phrases in sentences, essentially

speaking gibberish. I can't locate my vehicle in any parking lot, and you should eat my cooking at your own risk. Halfway through the process, my mind slipped elsewhere to tackle a problem and I cannot tell you what has gone into that pan.

These are warning signs to me. They're each a big red, flashing light signifying that I need to take a step back. My brain has gone into hyper-overdrive and is starting to malfunction. It's a bit unsettling, isn't it?

You probably have other warning signs, the invisible ones only you know about. Shoulders and neck aching from constant tension. A dull, unyielding headache. And, my personal favorite, grinding your teeth day and night. You'd think that physical pain would stop us in our tracks, but somehow we're able to trick ourselves into believing it's a separate issue. It's preferable to think we simply slept in a strange position rather than admit we're coming a bit undone. We'll just pop a painkiller and keep going, right?

Or maybe you're like me and you've gone to the doctor, sure something is wrong, and it turns out that you're "so tired all the time" because you're regularly working until 2:00 a.m. Or your jaw hurts not because you have tetanus, but because your frenetic pace has you clenching day and night.

We almost prefer that everything physical is just that: physical, completely out of our control. We prefer to just pick up a prescription or assume there's nothing we can do—because evaluating our own choices and lifestyle is really uncomfortable. It's hard work. But there are times when our pain, our recurring problems, are physical manifestations of emotional issues. And there are times when our bodies are breaking, trying to tell us— maybe even screaming at us—that they need a break, rest, care.

We'd learned this with Jon. Within a week of dropping to one job and adding daily swimming and an earlier bedtime, he felt noticeable improvement. Not major improvement, but when you've been bottomed out for a year plus, improvement at all is a big deal. The connection between mind and body is real, and it's strong. We are one person, and it's dangerous to think of ourselves in dichotomous terms.

When we ignore our body's signals—the aching back or the inability to keep track of our keys—we're headed for disaster. Maybe it's undealt with emotional trauma, maybe it's a pace that never allows rest, or maybe it's tension from living under too much pressure. Whatever it is, your body is off-kilter and it's only going to get worse if you don't deal with the underlying issue. Your body might be tapping you on the shoulder now, trying to get your attention. But in a few months or a few years, that tap is going to grow into a full-on smack as the situation becomes more serious.

We don't have to wait for a medical meltdown or for years of unknowable symptoms—we can begin now to listen to our body, to pay attention to the warning signs. We can pause, evaluate. *Where do I need to pull back? Where am I over-extending myself? In what way am I dwelling in anxiety?*

It's been just as important for me in this process as it's been for Jon. Even with outward improvements, I hadn't really begun to recover internally. I was still on edge, still angry—at God, at myself, and at everyone. It took some pretty strong signals from my body to recognize how wound up I was, that I hadn't released the stress, the sadness.

While I could do without the occasional rash flare-up—and I'm sure none of us enjoys the ache of a tense jaw—these things can save us, if we'll just listen and respond.

LOOKING INWARD: What are your body's caution signals? How do you typically respond to them? What has worked well (or not well) in the past?

LOOKING UPWARD: Our God formed each one of us (Psalm 139:13–14). Praise him for his care in putting us together, in sustaining us, and for his desire to see us healthy and whole.

LOOKING OUTWARD: Divide a journal page into two columns. On the left side, list out your caution signs—tension headaches, irritability, sleeping through your alarm, losing your keys, grinding your teeth. On the right side, write out how you will respond when you see these signs: evaluate your schedule, check in on key relationships, visit your therapist, book a quiet morning alone.

Day 25

Happy Hearts

One of the greatest tragedies that can befall the modern woman is not having friends or family with whom she can be herself. No, not your cool self or humorous self or great-conversationalist self. I mean your burst-into-song, laugh-until-you-pee-your-pants self. With so much of life requiring poise and keeping up appearances, we absolutely need time to be uninhibited and free, to just have fun.

This quality ranks pretty high in our family ethos. In the Wise household, one is free to be as quirky and goofy and uninhibited as desired—it's encouraged. In our home, you will not be ridiculed for strange dance moves, singing at the top of your lungs, wearing a ramshackle outfit, or entering the room with a ballerina leap. If you can't be your free self with your family, then where can you?

This freedom is more common in childhood, but then you're an adult—and the fun is all rather polite, rather unfun in my opinion. This is something I'd complained about for years, ever since I left college and my love-you-like-my-sisters

wild and ridiculous roommates. Because those years were full of uninhibited, off-the-charts good times.

But then several years ago we chose a house in Bryn Mawr, sight unseen, and arrived a month later with all of our belongings. The house and street were a big change from our little town on a lake outside of Minneapolis. There it was quiet, slow. Here it's compact, loud, busy. Yet we quickly discovered that some of the people right on our block also happened to be some of our favorite people. It's almost uncanny—four families, all within a baby-monitor-range distance (hugely important for late nights on the patio) just clicked in a way that is sweet beyond words. The kids are a stepladder of ages. They play beautifully and love like siblings.

And very regularly we all get together—Christie and Justin, Janine and Stefano, Chris and Erika. Last-minute BBQs, progressive dinners, snow-day potlucks, bonfires where we toast any and all candy left stashed around our houses from the holidays. (Did you know you can toast Starbursts? Try it.) We have a pretty good thing going.

One of our first summers as friends we all made the trek out to the suburb where Christie and Justin had grown up to visit a very special place called The Tiki Bar. Allow me to paint a picture: during the warmer months, a small ski resort transforms its deck at the bottom of the hill into a Hawaiian-themed outdoor dining experience. I say "experience" because that's what it is. It's a locals-only vibe. The tableware is plastic. You choose and purchase your uncooked food at a meat counter and then grill it yourself on gigantic communal grills. Also important to note: there are vats of melted butter at the

grilling stations to liberally pour over the food while it chars. It's bizarre and unrefined and wonderful.

At the end of the night, we all crammed back into one car, and something happened. Maybe it was the result of spending the evening in such a strange and funny environment. Maybe it was the cramped back seat cutting off oxygen to our brains. But on our drive home, smooshed in the back seat together, we laughed and whooped and belted out "MMMBop" with abandon. I had a flashback to college, smooshed into the front seat of Amy's little tan truck with Rachel, Kristina, and Lydia, blaring Jimmy Eat World and singing at the top of our lungs—and I knew in that moment that I hadn't had friends like these in a really long time.

This is huge. Because sometimes life is boring, or it's bleak—your kids won't sleep through the night, or a coworker is out to get you, or your marriage is unraveling. Sometimes you can go days, weeks, without more than a friendly smile or a polite chuckle—when what will really do your heart good is laughing until your abs ache. We need fun. We need cheer. We need happiness.

Somehow, happiness has gotten a bad rap. You can almost feel shamed for seeking happiness. Happiness, some will say, is shallow. It's true that happiness is temporary, situational—whereas we can choose and dwell in joy in any circumstance. Yes, joy is so great. So important. But let's not discount or forget the power of a happy heart.

Proverbs 17:22 (NLT) tells us, "A cheerful heart is good medicine, but a broken spirit saps a person's strength." And earlier, in chapter 15, "For the despondent, every day brings trouble; for the happy heart, life is a continual feast" (Proverbs

jumped up in excitement, stamping muddy footprints all over my clothes. I jumped back, startled. And then I apologized.

"Oops! Sorry!"

The woman gave her dog a tug and went on her way. I wanted to slap myself.

What on earth was I apologizing for? That her dog jumped on me? That I was on the path? That I had the audacity to go for a walk with my friend on a gorgeous day? That I existed at all?

I was just as bothered by my own apology as I was by her lack of one—mostly because it pointed to a larger problem: I tend to take responsibility for other people's actions. This plays out in my constant apologies for things like muddy paw prints or when someone walks straight into me ("Sorry!" I say when someone rudely knocks into me). And it also plays out when anyone seems unhappy with me, ever, for any reason.

I'm uneasy when someone appears stern. I loathe disappointing anyone. I become anxious if I've upset someone, even if it wasn't my fault. I can worry for months if it seems my intentions have been misunderstood. I may even mentally return to one of these events years later. It's a sickness, friends.

And just as it wears on me, it wears me out. Because I'll bend over backward and bleed myself dry tying to appease the angry, uplift the perpetually irritable. If I think someone is upset with me, I'll just keep putting myself out there—trying to connect with a joke, flashing warm smiles, sending all the "I'm nice. I like you. Please just like me back" signals I can.

The thing is, sometimes I should just move on. Because, if I'm misunderstood, or if someone just simply doesn't like

me (gasp), my obsessing isn't healthy or helpful. There's no good that comes from dancing around like a circus clown trying to gain everyone's goodwill. I'm learning that all I can bear responsibility for is my own actions, my own attitude. I've gotten better at it—but it's not easy.

As we struggled through Jon's recovery, I found myself in an awkward relationship with a woman from church. She had befriended me shortly after we moved to the area—we had kids close in age and it made sense that we'd get together from time to time. Yet as the months ticked on I began to feel like half friend, half human life support. I liked her; however, her level of emotional need was more than one person could fulfill. One day she might call for an impromptu forty-five minute ride home from the car mechanic; two days later she might text for a companion to come sit on her couch simply to feel less lonely.

When we'd first met I was happy to help. She was overwhelmed, struggling, unhappy in her marriage, looking for friendship. And these are the things friends do, right? But after a while I began to wear out. The asks were unending, the needs insatiable. And if I was unable to comply, I was met with a guilt trip and dramatic disappointment. Eventually I'd give in.

You might be thinking, "Stop being friends!" But I didn't want to cut this person out of my life, and at the time, we attended the same church. Our paths would continue to cross. I couldn't bear the thought of mingling through coffee hour in the same room, seeing the veiled accusations in her eyes. Yet with all we were wading through with Jon's health and our own life changes, I simply couldn't keep her afloat as well. Something had to change.

I had to stop worrying about this woman's opinion of me. She and I had different views of what makes a good friend, and while I could continue to be a friend, it would have to be with boundaries in place. I needed to be confident in my decisions, and not waver when she expressed her displeasure.

I'd love to tell you that after a few months of this she learned to recognize healthy boundaries, but that's not the case. In the end, she cut me from her life without warning. I know that she misunderstood my boundaries for unkindness, for not including, for rude behavior. And that bothered me. A lot. And boy, was I tempted to start dancing and clapping, trying to convince her that I'm not a bad person. But I didn't. Because we can't live our lives as people pleasers.

It's difficult, right? It's difficult when you know the other person is writing their own narrative. So difficult when you know that the other person is shaping her opinion of you based on her own struggles. So difficult when this person is in your church or neighborhood—and you know her tinted view is possibly tinting others' views of you too. But there is health and freedom when we can claim responsibility for our own actions and not someone else's.

Sometimes we just have to let go of the fact that someone doesn't like us. Sometimes we have to just be okay that the lady across the street has a strange impression of us. Sometimes we have to stop trying to make someone happy who simply isn't.

Because when we live our lives to please people, we'll never be off the hook. Proverbs 29:25 warns, "The fear of human opinion disables; trusting in God protects you from that" (MSG). When we're constantly trying to make everyone

happy, make sure everyone likes us, we'll never get anywhere. We'll run out of energy simply from saying yes to every request, going out of our way to boost other's opinions of us, and scrambling to put a smile on every face.

As hard as it may be, we need to release the fear of being disliked or misunderstood. We can be kind, we can be gracious, we can love like Christ—all things that please God, bring honor to his name. And then we can stop the circus act and let others be responsible for their own actions, their own attitudes. Because our lives aren't about human approval—we answer to God alone, and we know that he finds delight in us (Psalm 149:4). That's the only approval needed.

LOOKING INWARD: Who are you trying to please? Where are you spending yourself out of a fear of being disliked? Do you find yourself worrying about other's opinions of you?

LOOKING UPWARD: Commit your trust to God, to finding your approval in him. Ask him for wisdom and peace as you navigate awkward situations, difficult relationships, and healthy boundaries. Praise him for the comfort he brings.

LOOKING OUTWARD: Identify one way you're performing in order to gain someone's approval. In your journal, write out what it could look like to move forward with grace and kindness, but no need to gain approval.

Day 27

We Need You

I'm consumed with checking the weather, looking at flight times, researching hotels, and coordinating with friends and family members, all in an attempt to actually slip away for a bit of respite.

Last week while zipping along an online hotel search, I paused briefly to read a few reviews of the top candidates. Breezing through, I saw the usual range of responses; however, two in particular caught my eye. Two different reviewers had stayed at the exact same hotel, on the exact same night, each traveling alone with a child, but their responses couldn't have been more different.

From the first reviewer: "The noise from the rooftop band was intolerable. . . . We should have been warned. We will never stay at this hotel again."

From the second reviewer: "My daughter and I loved our room. It had a spectacular view of a rooftop concert. Our stay will be cherished for years to come—thank you."

I shook my head. It reminded me of so much feedback I've observed and experienced over the years. If you organize an

event, one person will say, "Everyone loved it! We *have* to do this again!" and another will tell you, "It was so overcrowded! Everyone was miserable!" If you buy organic food, one person will think you're neurotic, while another will chastise you for still using "regular" shampoo. Depending on who we're with, we can be perceived as too uptight or too laid-back, too unkempt or too vain, too boring or too wild, too outspoken or too insecure. And the list goes on.

It's so easy to slip into trying to fit whatever people think we should be. At a networking function we might feel the need to prove our professionalism, put together an outfit that looks accomplished, or name-drop former clients. While chatting with other parents, we feel pressured to proudly state how little "screen time" is allowed in our homes, the millions of activities our children are balancing, and all the ways we're providing a sweet, wholesome environment. When out with girlfriends, we're suddenly aware of whether we're going on dates enough, hitting the gym enough, taking care of our hair, skin, makeup, and closet enough.

This pressure to be everything to everyone is exhausting, and somewhere along the line we need to acknowledge a couple things. First, it is impossible to be what everyone wants us to be, in part because "everyone" cannot even agree on what that is. Second, it's far more important to hold true to who we're created to be than it is to try to fit into someone else's expectations.

Check out this example of John the Baptist and Jesus, found in Luke 7. "John the Baptizer came fasting and you called him crazy. The Son of Man came feasting and you called him a lush. Opinion polls don't count for much, do

they? The proof of the pudding is in the eating" (Luke 7:33–35 MSG).

Isn't it fascinating to see that public opinion doesn't play fair for anyone?

The people who criticized John the Baptist for his strict diet were the very same people who criticized Jesus for eating and drinking and hanging out with questionable characters. And this wasn't just your run-of-the-mill gossip and rude-comments type of criticism. But here's the thing: neither of them changed course. They didn't make adjustments to make people happy. They didn't worry about ways to appear more "normal." They didn't bend in order to fit in.

Both Jesus and John the Baptist held steady, true to their God-given identity and God-ordained calling, even amidst the fiercest persecution.

That looks a little different for each one of us. Some of us are outgoing and funny and love in big ways; some of us are quiet, wholehearted, and kind. Some of us are drawn to a nine-to-five and a calm routine; some of us feel squelched without risk. Some of us love to cast a big vision; some of us love to pour ourselves into the details of making that vision reality.

We do ourselves, and the world, a disservice when we try to be anything but ourselves. Each of us is made with a unique mix of strengths, interests, capabilities. Each of us wakes each day with a unique history, outlook, passion. Each of us holds a space in this world, a space in God's mission to spread love, bring healing, and restore this world. When we hide, exagger-ate, or twist who we are, we leave our space vacant. Who will be you, while you're off trying to be someone else?

It doesn't matter if you're professional enough, outgoing enough, proper enough, wild enough. You are enough. And we need you, in your perfect makeup or no makeup at all, your over-the-top romantic marriage or your comfortable partnership, your skyrocketing career or your just-right job. You hold a unique place in this world—and a unique place in the hearts and lives of your friends, family, and neighbors.

God created you with care and intention. Don't waiver; don't shy away from who you are. You are a part of the family of God—with the purpose of working together to bless our world. We can't do it without you. The real you.

Let's shine brightly just as God made us, unashamed and unwavering. Let's shrug off the confinement of other people's expectations and confidently press forward into our identity as God's children. And let's find that when we stop trying to be everything else, we can be exactly who we want to be: ourselves.

LOOKING INWARD: In what ways do you bend, or represent yourself differently, in order to try to fit in and measure up? How has God made you unique? What is the calling before you?

LOOKING UPWARD: Praise God for his creativity, his care, the way he makes each of us unique. Thank him for the way he made you, gifted you, and calls you. Confess the times you've shied away from being yourself, doubting his work and his hand in your life, and ask for his help in living into your unique, God-given identity.

LOOKING OUTWARD: Grab a journal and divide the page into three sections. In the first, list your unique abilities, skills, and strengths. In the second section, record the work before you—tangible work, such as your job and family responsibilities, but also the work that's been laid on your heart, the issues and people to whom you feel called. In the final section, prayerfully explore what it means for you, with your unique abilities, personality, and experiences, to carry out your work and respond to your calling. Return to this practice often as you uncover new talents and opportunities.

Day 28

Internal Trash Critic

As a rule, I don't speak badly about my husband, but I can't hold this one in. I was so mad. A few days ago—you won't believe this—he bagged up and removed the trash from the upstairs bathroom. I cannot tell you how hotly my blood boiled. The second I saw him carrying that bag toward the door it took all of my effort to not make a scene. Except that I still made a scene.

I get it. The trash was full. It should never be full. And since I'm the one who primarily takes care of the home, it was my fault that it hadn't been emptied yet. Our house should always be spotless. Clearly, I was a couple days late on cleaning the bathroom, just as I'm late on a hundred other items, because I'm not on top of things and I'm failing not just at the bathroom trash, but failing at life.

His response? "I saw that it was full and so I emptied it." Pretty flimsy.

It took a full day for me to calm down from this trash-removing incident, only to be haunted with a lingering thought: was it possible that he had truly just been taking out the trash instead of commenting on my ability to properly maintain a home, or worse, my life? Was it possible that his look of bewilderment was genuine? Could it be that the accusations that cut so deeply hadn't come from him at all, but rather from myself?

So often our own insecurity is the root of our problems. If we're honest with ourselves, we can probably find a correlation between our deepest insecurities and what we perceive as the veiled accusations of others. If we're insecure about our body image, we may perceive a shy salesperson as slighting us because of our weight. If we feel insecure about our educational level, we may perceive our spouse's difference of opinion as a comment on our intelligence. And if we are insecure about our ability to do everything perfectly, all the time, we might just have a meltdown when someone takes out the trash.

It's difficult to find someone who is more judgmental of us than ourselves. Not only that, the pressure and expectations that we place on ourselves tend to far exceed the ones coming from anyone else. How does this happen? Why is it that we're our own biggest critics—our own worst enemies?

I know that I have crazy expectations for myself, but I still struggle to let them go. Somewhere along the line I developed this idea that I need to have everything in order, I can't make any mistakes. This goes for items big and small—I can feel just as much shame at a leftover coffee cup in my car as I could feel if I missed a work deadline or forgot to pay our water bill. Even as I type this I'm fighting an internal battle over my chipped nail polish. Everything in me screams that this chipped polish isn't okay, and more than that—that I'm not okay.

Yet we usually don't expect the same level of perfection from others, right? If someone else burnt a recipe, forgot to attach a file to an email, or knocked over a coffee mug, it wouldn't even register as an event. When I'm the one walking around with coffee on my shirt, all I can think is one thing: I'm a failure.

On top of this, it's easy to beat ourselves up when we're so keenly aware of our actual faults. We know every misstep, every unkind thought, every regret. We see missed opportunities, hear judgmental words slip from our lips, and hold onto the past. And we refuse to let go of the guilt that plagues us.

But if we trust in Jesus we have no reason to carry this load. We know that "as far as the east is from the west, so far has he removed our transgressions from us" (Psalm 103:12). None of us is perfect, but the good news is that God knows this, and he loves us as we are. We don't need to be hindered by guilt and shame, caught in insecurity—we can approach God with confidence, knowing we'll receive mercy, grace, help (Hebrews 4:16).

Our insecurities will shrink as we grow in our identity as children of God and learn to rest in his grace. We don't have to try so hard. We don't have to measure up to our own, or anyone else's, standards. The only person we answer to is God, and we already have his love and acceptance 100 percent. There is nothing we can do to earn it or lose it. Let's embrace this—live in it.

Let's make a conscious decision to give ourselves a break. Go crazy: don't make the bed, allow yourself to be late occasionally, forgive yourself for an unkind word, and stop obsessing in the mirror. Because when we learn to be steeped in grace, we'll begin to see it poured out for others as well.

Next time someone says something that seems fraught with accusations, let's step back and honestly consider whose voice we're hearing. I think we'll be surprised to find it's often our own. Let's allow these moments to initiate some healing of our self-inflicted emotional wounds, and we'll find our relationships rejuvenated and made whole in the process.

LOOKING INWARD: What criticisms do you regularly lob at yourself? In what areas do you feel that you're coming up short? Think through some recent interpersonal conflicts, times you've been offended or upset—do you hear any of your own voice coming through?

LOOKING UPWARD: Meditate on God's grace for you. Spend a moment considering his love and acceptance for you—even when you don't love or accept yourself. Ask God to help in extending grace for yourself, which will overflow to the people you love.

LOOKING OUTWARD: Consider your regular self-criticisms, and choose one to tackle first. Commit to releasing its hold on you and on your relationships. Find a Bible verse that speaks directly to this critique, or try Psalm 138:8. Post it on your mirror, your dashboard, or as the wallpaper on your phone—read it aloud throughout the day. When the self-accusations begin, pause and remind yourself, "I am a Child of God. I am enough."

Day 29

Traverse City

I started smiling as soon as we could smell the bay water. Summertime had arrived again, and we'd again slipped away to Traverse City. As we pulled into town, we swapped the air conditioning for open windows, allowing the intoxicating fresh air to breeze through. Home.

We were several months into our attempt at a more restful, healthful, trusting lifestyle. Jon's pain levels continued to diminish with some ups and downs. And we continued to decompress from the stress of it all, with some ups and downs.

Now here we were back in Traverse City for another summer, a full year since the previous summer when we were hobbling along, awaiting the doctor's appointment that would change everything. It was almost hard to comprehend how much had happened in that time, how much we'd changed, how different our lives felt. We always appreciated the separateness of Traverse City, the unique rhythm of the city, the way of life—but now we saw its value through new eyes.

Life is different in Traverse City. People hold jobs, build careers, take children to activities, and participate in all the

normal events of contemporary life. Yet the assumed pace is different; the values are different. There's much more biking and much less sitting in traffic. Much more inspired local food, much less generic chain restaurants. Much more bonfire on the beach, much less working around the clock.

I know what you're thinking—it's vacation; everyone is relaxed and has fun on vacation. But that's not it. Yes, we leave a certain amount of expectations and commitments behind when we head west on 76, but we're still us. We still bring along workloads, deadlines, kids' activities, and the normal day-to-day responsibilities.

One morning as our children set sail on Boardman Lake (for sailing camp, not unsupervised—please don't call CPS), Jon and I settled in at Blk Mrkt, our most loved coffee shop in town. We talked over iced coffees and their famous hand pies, ruminating on what made this place so special.

"I think people here just enjoy life more," Jon said. Having grown up there, I had to agree.

Recreation is just as much a natural part of the week as work, doing your laundry, or grocery shopping. Finished eating dinner at seven? Rather than flipping open your laptop or lounging in front of the television for the next four hours, how about a bike ride, a walk through downtown, or a quick swim in the bay?

Care and intentionality are given for details that are often skipped over in other places. Local, fresh, healthy food reigns supreme. Art and beauty are abundant. The earth is treasured and tended. Community is king.

When we're in Traverse City, we don't work in the evenings. We go on long bike rides on the weekends and make

the most of days off. We sprawl out on my parents' deck, relaxing in the breeze, listening to the rustling leaves, watching the chipmunks raid the bird feeder.

When we're back home, free time doesn't feel free—maybe we could sneak in a quick email or two. When we're back home, weekends aren't for enjoying—we need to reset for another week of productivity. When we're back home, we fall into the pressures and pace of our culture. But what if we resisted? What if we lived Traverse City back on the East Coast? What if our summer detox became our year-round rhythm?

Most of us wade through our weekly rhythms with an eye toward our next chance to slip away. Our day-to-day life is mundane, exhausting, and uninspired—we just need to hang on for the next vacation where we can slow down, eat better food, get more sleep, and spend time with people we love. It's a jolt of goodness, yet we return home and jump right back into the frenzy.

The thing is, these days, the regular ones where we scramble and sweat and crash into bed at night, they make up our life far more than the random long weekends away. A few days of rest and recreation aren't going to change your emotional health in the same way that a weekend at a health spa isn't going to change your past six months of overeating. We're looking to create a way of life, not a short-term escape.

What if we didn't need a summer detox? What if our yearlong, nonvacation, day-in-and-day-out life was healthy, vibrant, fresh? I mean, I'd still go to Traverse City for the summer. You can't take that away from me—I need to see the friends and family I love, I need to splash in the fresh water,

and I need to eat all the food. But still—how incredible would it be to return home without having the wind knocked out of us?

Could we cancel the cable, begin an evening routine of a family walk around the block, plan a half day of recreation and relaxation every weekend? What if we just sat outside and let the breeze wash over us? What if we snuggled up with a family member and read a book together, a chapter per morning? Let's try cooking a fresh, seasonal meal. Let's step away from the home improvement projects from time to time.

We may not be able to live this perfectly, but every morning offers a fresh start, a new chance to try again, live the life we want, the one we were meant for. Lamentations 3:22–23 says, "Because of the Lord's great love we are not consumed, for his compassions never fail. They are new every morning; great is your faithfulness."

We can always start over. Every morning, any morning. It's never too late to step out of the rat race, say farewell to frenzied, and dive further into God's compassion and faithfulness that offer forgiveness, rest, and abundant new horizons.

LOOKING INWARD: What's your favorite place to slip away, relax, enjoy, and connect with loved ones? What makes it special? What's different there, enabling you to live a few days of a healthy pace, a few days of nobler values?

LOOKING UPWARD: God's mercies are new every single day. It's not too late to live a life that is vibrant, that celebrates the good gifts in the ordinary. Thank God for his compassion, for his forgiveness that wipes the slate clean, for his desire that we enjoy this world he created for us.

LOOKING OUTWARD: What would it look like to infuse your regular, day-to-day life with some rhythms and elements of your favorite hideaway? Brainstorm some practical, real-life ideas. Then put at least one into practice this week.

Day 30

Go Small and Go Home

One bonus of attending seminary is having roommates with whom you can seamlessly discuss both theology and dating. And discuss we did. Dawn, Hannah, Yoon, and I covered a lot of ground both in our talks over the finer points of theology and over the finer men on campus. One subject of our discussions was Chad.

Chad and I spent time together—think more than friends, less than dating. This in-between space, this had always been my sweet spot. I could crush all I wanted, enjoy the fun of flirting and the perks of a cute guy's attention, but without the baggage of a committed relationship. (Yes, I hear it. Apparently I was a terrible person.)

But Chad wasn't so much an in-between-space guy. He was focused and serious about dating. He wasn't just flirting, he was looking for a wife. So it was just a month or so in when he wanted to have "the talk."

Where was this going? Well, nowhere. We both knew it, but I was the only one who was comfortable with that. Chad's take? "Go big or go home." That's a direct quote. I remember

distinctly because I found it so annoying. What was wrong with this easy, no-strings-attached in-between?

For all my eye-rolling, it turned out to be the right call. Just a couple short weeks later I met Jon, who was attending music school in the city, and within twenty-four hours we were fully in Go Big territory. He proposed three months later, and four months after that we celebrated our marriage back in Traverse City among friends and family, overlooking the bay.

And here we were now on the worse side of "for better or for worse"—on the sickness side of "in sickness and in health." But we were moving along together and we were inching toward health, hoping for better. Every day required tough choices. Every day required intentionality and discipline. There was no going with the flow—we'd already learned that the flow is more of an undertow, and we preferred to stay afloat.

Every few days we'd need to evaluate an invitation, an idea, a project. Did we have time? Did we have energy? Did this match up with our highest values and goals? How would it impact our family rhythm and health?

Sometimes there was no easy answer. Sometimes it was complicated. Sometimes I froze when I needed to move forward, unable to choose a next step.

I was in precisely that spot when Dawn came to visit. We hadn't seen one another in over a decade, in which time she had earned two more degrees, lived and loved in Iraq, married, and brought a daughter into the world. She traveled from Redding, California, with her family, and we picked up right where we had left off. Except, instead of agonizing over the merits of our male classmates, I now agonized over life and career choices. What do I hold on to, what do I let go?

That particular week I had been dragging my feet on making a decision. I was committed to attending a preaching conference in Michigan in a few weeks and had not yet purchased airfare. The conference was at Western Seminary, just a couple-hour drive from my grandfather. If I stayed the rest of the week, I could sneak in a good visit. This gave this trip high value—it was a rare chance to spend time with my family, especially since I lived so far away. I wanted to capitalize on this opportunity. It was good to do this.

However, Breckin's birthday was that Saturday. If you have kids, you know that a child's birthday is not just a matter of one day. There's the birthday party with friends, the family celebration, the visit to the classroom to read and distribute favors, wrapping gifts, blowing up balloons, making a special breakfast, special dinner, special dessert. It's quite an ordeal and I knew there was no way to return Friday and fully celebrate without sending everything into chaos. This option also had high value: creating special moments and memories for my children, building into their sense of being valued and loved. I wanted to shower Breckin with birthday love. It was good to do this.

I liked the sound of both. I highly valued both. I would enjoy both. Unfortunately, it would be impossible to do both. I laid out my options to Dawn—I either stay in Michigan and enjoy some rare quality time with my grandpa, or I fly straight back and avoid creating a stressful sequence of events at home.

"What I'm learning," she said, "is that sometimes you can't do everything, but you can do something." She suggested

staying just one additional day, thus enabling me to see my grandfather and be home to make Breckin's birthday special.

It made sense—but I couldn't shake the idea that stopping in for one day together wasn't all right. It wasn't a legit visit. Surely no visit was better than this too-fast-to-be-meaningful visit. It felt embarrassing to only come for one day.

And yet I knew it was what I had to give.

When the time came, it did feel short. I did wish I had more time. But the day was special. And meaningful. And I can't believe I almost missed the opportunity because it didn't meet my own standard of being enough.

Maybe sometimes we can't go big, but that doesn't mean we have to go home, either. Maybe we don't have the bandwidth to attend our neighbor's birthday dinner, but we could drop flowers and a card on her porch the next morning. Maybe we can't join the church Bible study, but we could read along with our morning coffee on our own schedule. Maybe we can't plan the holiday party at work, but we can pay for the cupcakes.

Maybe it doesn't have to be about how much we do, but why we do it, and that we do something at all.

We'd all like to lob impressive, attention-grabbing confetti balls of blessing and care all day long, but we don't need to be embarrassed or shy away when we don't have the time, energy, or bandwidth.

Can we do this—find the smaller, more doable version of the grand-scale gesture we imagine? Giving what we actually have to give rather than overextending ourselves or becoming discouraged and doing nothing at all?

Let's shrug off the self-imposed pressure to go big, and let's not be embarrassed into going home. Send that quick encouragement text, donate water bottles for the class party—let's confidently give what we have to give, nothing more, nothing less.

LOOKING INWARD: Reflect on the past few months. When did you "go big," exceed your bandwidth, and end up regretting it? When did you "go home" and end up regretting it? How does the "go big or go home" mentality creep into your thoughts? What would it look like, practically, to let it go—to confidently engage the people and tasks around you with what you have to offer, nothing more, nothing less?

LOOKING UPWARD: Praise God for his infinite wisdom—that he far exceeds us in understanding. Ask him to help you discern when you can give a lot, and when you can give a little—and to graciously accept your own human limitations.

LOOKING OUTWARD: Brainstorm a few ways you can care for and engage the people in your life without overextending yourself—set a plan to give it a try. Text a friend to let her know you're thinking of her; offer to bring a beverage to a party rather than cooking.

Day 31

Heavenly Treasure

My sense of gratitude and contentment is embarrassingly unstable. It can swing all over the place in the course of a day or a week. Sometimes I'm so thankful for such great friends, healthy children, my adorable neighborhood gym, a kitchen full of food, my sweetest husband—I mean, stars are just floating around my head and sunshine beams from my eyes.

And then there are the other times. You know. When you can't find anything to wear because you have nothing to wear. Or when everything would just be easier if you could afford more help around the house or a nicer car or a professional decorator. Or when you wish your kids or spouse would just try more. These are not pretty moments. There are no floating stars. Just a whiny, spoiled me, moping about my day's tasks.

Please tell me you've experienced this too. I'm sure I'm not alone here.

As it turns out, when we find our contentment in having enough, being enough, or looking good enough, it's so easy to steal. One bad hair day, one step into a friend's picture-perfect home, one Facebook update about an old classmate's rocketing career, and it's gone. This is a dangerous way to live.

This must be what Jesus is talking about when he warns of thieves in Matthew 6. Earthly treasure rusts, it's corroded, it's eaten by moths and stolen away from us. Heavenly treasure, we're assured, is safe and sound. It's not going to flit away when we realize someone else has more or better.

So why do we continue to try to find comfort in the things we know will fail us? Maybe it's because we're inundated with advertising—to be honest, no matter how diligent I am at unsubscribing from lists and tossing catalogues directly into the recycling bin, I still quickly fall prey to a sidebar on my computer screen that proclaims, "Additional 30% Off Sale Prices!" at my favorite stores. Surely there is something I need at 30 percent off the sale price. Maybe I can finally dress nicer, fit in better, and buy some confidence in the form of a really cute dress.

Maybe it's because we do "the scan" every time we encounter someone new. We all do it. We're introduced to someone at a party or work function and perform a quick once-over to see exactly what she has that we're missing. I have literally engaged in a sixty-second interaction with someone and walked away with a mental list of everything I'm "lacking." (Of course, I just didn't know I was lacking these things until now. Thank you, new friend, for helping me see my lowliness.)

These experiences are rust; they're moths. And our gratitude and contentment needs to be found in a different kind of treasure—treasure that isn't susceptible to these predators. We store up treasure in heaven when we value relationships

over things, when we focus on our hearts over our appearance, and when we choose to live a life deeply steeped in God and his love for our world. And here's a bonus: we're not just storing up treasure for later, but for now. God is here now, and right now we get to enjoy the treasures of love, peace, community, and restoration.

Last Christmas Lauren put together a gift exchange for the six of us: her and Jesse, Stell and Richard, and Jon and me. We were each assigned a specific person and had a month or two to come up with a gift. Between the creative, dynamic personalities, our many shared inside jokes, and our keen knowledge of one another's quirks, this was sure to be a fairly epic gift exchange. Each of us accepted the challenge and thought long and hard about what to give. It was fun, but it was work. After brainstorming, shopping, panicking, crafting, and shopping some more, we showed up at Lauren's house one night in late December with oddities in tow.

We enjoyed a stunning spread of cheeses, truffle honey (a Lauren cheese-plate staple—bless her heart), and fruit and seedy crackers, and then the gift giving commenced. It was truly incredible. While you may never give or receive things like a miniature party barn or loafers carved out of Whole Foods multigrain bread, these things made us laugh until we cried—and these things made my heart overflow.

As the holidays passed and we rounded the new year, I couldn't stop thinking of gift ideas for our next exchange. It was almost a year away, but what had required so much effort to see before was now everywhere I looked. Each time we met for dinner, chatted after church, or engaged in some snarky six-way text thread, gift ideas shot off like fireworks

in my mind. This is why in February I was already tracking down things like a gasoline-scented candle, a Jabbawockeez mask, and a costume to match Katy Perry's "Chained to the Rhythm" Grammy performance.

Because once we've truly gotten a taste of something good, and once we're accustomed to looking for it, it's always so much easier to see. This is exactly how gratitude works. Psalm 34:8 tells us to "taste and see that the Lord is good." I really believe that once our gratitude is rooted in his goodness, his care for us, his love, that we'll begin to spot it everywhere. We'll see it in the richest, darkest cup of coffee, in the kind text from a friend who knows it's been a long week, in the breeze rustling on a hot summer day. The goodness of God is prevalent all around us, if we have eyes to see it—and this is one treasure that can't be stolen.

Let's turn our eyes away from getting more and being more. Let's recognize and celebrate God's goodness, and all that he has given to us. Let's set our hearts on heavenly treasure, where we find genuine gratitude—the kind that lasts.

LOOKING INWARD: Do you struggle to feel consistently content? What are the "moths" and "rust" in your life—what steals your gratitude?

LOOKING UPWARD: Offer up to God an honest confession. Confess the earthly treasures that you value over the heavenly treasures he offers.

LOOKING OUTWARD: Open a note page in your phone and begin a thank you note to God. Try to commit to an entire week. Throughout the day, add items for which you're thankful—a smooth commute, a friendly barista, a funny text, a bird outside your window. It may take intentionality at first, but over time it will become a natural instinct to feel gratitude and offer thanks to the Lord.

Day 32

Complicated

*B*reckin declares his jealousy over our dog's life on a biweekly basis. Usually it's in the morning before school, when he'll glance up from his breakfast to spot her snoozing in her bed, and say, "Gidgit is so lucky. I wish I was a dog. She just gets to sleep in and do whatever she wants."

I've tried pointing out that while she does, in fact, get to sleep as much as she likes, she's not exactly getting to do much of excitement or interest throughout the day. For starters, she's very old and tired. Additionally, without opposable thumbs the world really isn't her oyster. I'm not sure she's living a life worth envying.

Ironically, as he's sitting at the table envying the ease of the dog's life, I'm often sitting across from him and Ellington envying the ease of theirs. Sure, they're about to go to school for the day. But compared to my adult life, it seems they can sleep in and do whatever they want.

They don't have to think, "What are we having for dinner tonight?" They simply have to show up at the table. They don't have to worry about getting laundry done or house repairs or

budget conversations. Their weekends are theirs to simply roll into at their own leisure.

Simplicity is what I miss most about being a kid. I know some of us experienced hardship or trauma as a child—but generally speaking, those younger years feel safer, more secure. Relatively easy and carefree. We weren't yet worried about appearances, we didn't have to hustle to keep up, we weren't buried under a growing list of to-dos and responsibilities.

And for those of us who grew up in the church, even our faith felt simpler. When I was younger I knew God loved me, I knew Jesus provided forgiveness of my sins, and I knew that the Spirit lived inside me. This was it. This was enough.

My parents would pray with us every night. Bless their hearts for not squelching our long and, I'm sure, repetitive prayers. We never felt that our prayers needed to impress. We just knew we could open our hearts to God. We never questioned if God hears our prayers, if our prayers matter, or the theology of God's providence. We just knew he wanted to hear from us, he cared. Simple.

Similarly, we didn't question God's forgiveness. I never wondered if God really loved me—of course he did, he said he did. I never wondered if he would forgive me—of course he did, he said he would. I knew I wasn't perfect, but I knew I was perfectly loved. Perfectly forgiven and made clean. Simple.

Somewhere along the line though things change. We bump into some harsh realities about other people's expectations, we come face-to-face with variant and conflicting opinions, we find ourselves under all sorts of pressure to perform and perfect someone else's version of a Christian

life. Suddenly it's not so simple anymore, and we launch into adulthood with a tangle of spiritual baggage, bogged down from the weight of it all.

Resting in God's love and forgiveness doesn't cut it anymore. A good Christian needs to begin every morning with extended Bible study and prayer. A good Christian needs to be in church several days a week, serving on multiple volunteer teams, and attending any offering that promises to be deep. A good Christian ensures her children know and use Christian jargon, memorize copious amounts of Scripture, and feel comfortable praying out loud in front of church groups. A good Christian always smiles, never yells, always gives, and never gets tired of it.

We make faith too complicated. We may even deceive ourselves into thinking that our spiritual life is deeper, more holy, if we attend all of the events, learn all of the theology, and master the art of thoughtful premeal prayers. But we couldn't be more wrong. When the disciples were arguing over who would rank highest in God's kingdom, Jesus says this: "I'm telling you, once and for all, that unless you return to square one and start over like children, you're not even going to get a look at the kingdom, let alone get in. Whoever becomes simple and elemental again, like this child, will rank high in God's kingdom" (Matthew 18:3–4 MSG).

Remember when we weren't obsessed with proving ourselves? Remember when we didn't worry about if we were doing enough to keep God happy? Remember when we could rest in God's love without a mental tick list of religious to-dos? We can return to those simpler times, simpler ways. We can return to square one.

This doesn't mean that we should halt any "religious" related activities. Volunteering in our churches, serving meals to the hungry, studying our Bibles—these are all good things. These are enriching and natural practices in the Christian life. But when we try to place our security, value, and our identity as God's children in our ability to keep up a routine, rather than in Christ alone, we're carrying a burden too great, never intended for us. And all of this heavy lifting doesn't amount to anything in the end.

In fact, 1 Corinthians 13 reminds us that we can keep up our religious routine, impress our peers, teach Scripture, feed the poor, and yet if our actions are rooted in just that, actions, it's all worthless. We will never find rest in the routine. We will never find peace in these practices. These things can only be found in and through God. Paul points us to the source at the end of the chapter, "Trust steadily in God, hope unswervingly, love extravagantly. And the best of the three is love" (1 Corinthians 13:13 MSG).

Faith, hope, and love. It's simple. It's square one. Let's return to our roots. Let's start there.

LOOKING INWARD: In what ways has your faith become more complicated over the years? What factors have contributed to this excess baggage? What would it take for you to be able to release it?

LOOKING UPWARD: Name and confess the ways you try to save yourself, prove yourself, with your religious routine. Thank God for his forgiveness, for his mercy, and for his every-day, never-ending invitation to start anew.

LOOKING OUTWARD: First Corinthians 13:13 boldly declares that love is our greatest calling. Prayerfully consider what this means in your life. What does it look like for you to tangibly live out love? We're not looking for more religious responsibilities, but an outpouring of what God has given to you. Maybe you'll spend extra time reading to your child. Maybe you'll extend hospitality to someone. Maybe you'll show up to your usual volunteer position, but with a heart bursting with love, not striving for security. How will you live out love this week?

Day 33

Stepping into the Rain

Several years back, I traveled, somewhat on a whim, to New York City in the company of three strangers. It would sound better if I could tell you I was in college or taking a gap year, but no. I was an adult, married, with children back at home.

I'd been invited by one of the three, a woman named Suzanne, to join in the trip to a conference focused on ministry within cities, after she learned of a lunch mentor program I'd started in our local elementary school. Not knowing my travel companions and having never been to Manhattan, I said sure and booked my flight. (And regrettably, I talked Suzanne into staying at a hostel "for the experience.")

It was a great few days, in spite of sleeping in a cinder-block room on a plastic mattress. I learned a lot connecting with leaders of initiatives from cities all over North America. I felt a surge of energy for my work. And I fell in love with New York.

When I spoke with Jon on the phone on our last day I said, "Can I just send for my things? I want to move to New York."

"How does an hour south of New York sound? Jared just called. He and Monica want us to move to the East Coast to be a part of Liberti, the church they planted a couple years back."

And so we did.

Okay, it wasn't that simple. There was a lot of conversation. Prayer. Some tears. Some of me telling off Jared in my head for even presenting this idea, because our kids were already in school, and we'd already moved a couple times—I was tired of being the new person. Still, while a major move would be painful and tough in the short term, we knew that a couple years out we would be happier, have a richer life, and stronger community. That spring we packed up and drove east to our new life. Hello, Philadelphia.

It was absolutely the right choice. Yes, there were tough goodbyes. Yes, making a big move like that with a family is a lot of work. Yes, there was an adjustment period where we learned how to navigate around town, where to find groceries, to not be offended that no one on the sidewalk smiles back, and how to not hit the cars parked on our very tight street. It was a season of work, but it birthed a really beautiful life. (I'm sorry, Jared, for telling you off in my head. You were right.)

So much of life is like that, isn't it? Seasons of work, of facing the unknown, that often yield results that couldn't have been born any other way. Jared and Monica were no stranger to that, themselves. Several years earlier they had packed up their family and moved into a 700-square-foot apartment in South Philly to plant Liberti Church.

Those early days were tough work. They shared one bedroom with their firstborn, Brennan, and the second bedroom

served as the church's office. Monica describes the apartment as having had an intimate view of the city—the good, the bad, and the degenerate. They had launched completely into the unknown and had more on their plate than previously thought possible. The mice kept the home/church office "cozy" and often the last of their grocery budget was spent on that Sunday's communion bread. It was a tough season—but it was a season.

And just as God worked in and through Jared and Monica to start Liberti, God has worked in and through Liberti to bless Philadelphia—both in the Center City and Main Line neighborhoods. It's a church for the city, because God is for the city. It's a church of rich, meaningful community, because it's centered around a triune, relational God.

Jared and Monica would tell you that tougher times would return, come and go, as their lives, and the life of the church, had its ups and downs, big blessings and challenges. We all know what this is like, right? Some days and years are simpler, straightforward. Others require exponentially more of us. And even when we're so careful with our schedule, our time—even when we cease striving and start trusting—there will be seasons that are just tough.

Sometimes you'll still have to do hard things. Some seasons are going to just take it out of you. Sometimes you'll have to work into the night to meet a deadline. Sometimes you won't be able to get the time off you want for some time away. Sometimes you may need to pick up some side work to make ends meet.

When this happens, let's resist discouragement, resist feeling guilty over a fuller schedule, over a return to the faster pace we worked hard to leave behind. Neither rhythms of work and rest nor Sabbath are one size fits all. They're going to look different outwardly at different times, yet we can hold on to the same value, same hope, same trust in God, in our hearts. We can remain steady, even when it seems everything is shifting around us.

And the shifting will come. It's a guarantee. In John 16:33 we find Jesus telling the disciples, "I have told you these things, so that in me you may have peace. In this world you will have trouble. But take heart! I have overcome the world."

Trouble isn't a maybe. Hardship isn't reserved only for those who make poor choices. We live in a broken world—we will have trouble. But Jesus offers us peace—he has overcome the world—his promises stand. Take heart!

What about those times we knowingly step into a tough season—a big move, a new venture? Those times when we go back to school on the weekends or chase after a dream? Sometimes we'll be caught up in a storm, but other times we'll find ourselves stepping out, intentionally, into the rain. And even in these tumultuous times, we can continue to live out our faith in God's promise for restoration, we can continue to trust he'll be the one to set us—and this world—right. We can still live in his rhythms of grace.

Maybe even more so because when we feel caught, pinched, we desperately need the freedom of space and the gift of peace. And we need grace over guilt—knowing deep down that God will sustain us through a period of more effort, when our sweet schedule of rest and recreation gets taken over with late hours in the office, or helping with an ailing family member, or early mornings of laundry and

cooking and homework checking in order to fit in the second job. Sometimes our healthy rhythms won't look as obviously healthy—but we know that even then, Jesus is calling us to stop trying so hard, to simply walk by his side.

It might look different. It will probably feel a lot less luxurious. But even in the hard seasons we can live with rest, recreation—we can seek out life-giving practices. Maybe our only free time all day is a thirty-minute lunch break. Could we put away our phones and read a book? What about a brown bag and a stroll out in the fresh air? Maybe our marriage is unraveling, and we're fighting to piece together a future. Could we commit one early morning a week to sit with a trusted friend? Maybe every extra moment has been taken by trips to the doctor, making appointments, hours on the phone fighting with the insurance company. Could we give ourselves permission to back out of some other responsibilities for a time? To gain just a little bit of quiet, rest?

We can spend weeks, months, or years developing a healthy pace, healthy rhythms, a lovely schedule that keeps us balanced. But friends, let's make sure it's all based in God's promises, in our trust in him, because while the externals will need to shift from time to time—and some seasons will be simpler than others—we can have confidence in a God who never changes, never falters, and is always our solid ground.

LOOKING INWARD: When did you find yourself in the midst of a difficult, tumultuous seasons? How did it feel? Were you able to find a new rhythm of health and rest during that time? Was it difficult to continue to trust in God's promise to set things right?

LOOKING UPWARD: Praise the Lord for his grace to see us through the hard seasons of life. Thank him for his grace to come alongside and walk with us— to offer us companionship rather than criticism.

LOOKING OUTWARD: What is distinct about healthy living that is based on a deep trust in God and his promises? What internal or external differences do you notice? How does this look different, particularly in tougher or more rigorous seasons?

Day 34

Starting Small

Do you ever browse social media and begin to worry you're doing it all wrong? And by all, I mean all. I can quickly feel like I don't measure up. Usually it's a passing fear that I can release, but sometimes it sends me into motion—which almost always backfires.

Last year, after seeing an unbearable amount of photos of families out traveling and at events, I began to feel guilty. Obviously, good parents plan special family activities in advance rather than trying to squeeze in bits of fun at the last minute. Why didn't I ever take the time to do this? Surely we were all suffering. I purchased concert tickets for one of our favorite artists. Except, of course, later that day the new school calendar arrived in the mail with a glaring conflict for the same evening. As Mat Kearney played what I can only assume was an incredible concert, I sat in an elementary school cafeteria thinking that maybe it's okay to just sneak in something special here and there when you can.

Mostly, these experiences serve as anecdotes to defend my already-set ways. Sometimes though, there's more to it.

A few months ago, after spending time with a friend who is the ultimate bargain shopper, I decided I should be thriftier. The kids needed a few new clothes before the school year began, and I headed straight to a poppy, generic chain store where I swear every item was 40 percent off. After returning home, snipping off tags, and tossing everything in the wash, I felt great about how little I had spent. Except, of course, that very evening I ran across an article about that very store and its unethical business practices. Was it possible I had purchased clothing stitched by hands no bigger than my own sons' as I attempted to be more financially responsible?

I felt sick. This experience, like so many others, unveiled the magnitude and complexity of what we're up against. Even when we try to do the right thing, when we're trying to solve one problem we're often playing into another one, whether we know or not. Trying to balance financial responsibility and ethical buying habits is overwhelming on its own. *Who stitched those shoes? Wow, that indie shoe company is way out of our budget! Are those chickens really free to roam? But whoa, those farmers' market eggs are expensive!*

And this is just a portion of the burden we feel. We are acutely aware of the overlapping issues of crime, safety, rehabilitation, racism, education, wealth disparity, privilege, and public health. Each of these issues is massive on its own, and when we realize the ways they play into one another, finding a solution can seem insurmountable.

It's all just so overwhelming. We can't see a way forward when the brokenness is all encompassing.

We see this dynamic in the book of Nehemiah.

The story picks up after the Babylonian exile when a portion of the Jews return to Jerusalem. They're home, but their problems aren't over yet. The city walls are crumbled, leaving them susceptible to a multitude of threats. The city would never be safe and rejuvenated until the walls were restored.

We can assume most of the returning Jews were already weary by this point. I know how worn out I am after a long trip, when just the thought of unpacking the suitcase sends me diving under the covers. So maybe they felt something like that, but times a zillion. And I can't even begin to imagine how daunting a project of this size would feel to this long-misplaced people.

Yet, as Nehemiah begins to organize the efforts in chapter 3, he does something extraordinary: he starts small. For those who lived in Jerusalem, those who had been in exile, those who had journeyed home only to find it in ruins, Nehemiah offers them an accessible starting point. While outsiders were given broader tasks, those who lived within the city were to repair the portion of the wall in front of their own homes.

The end of this chapter reads like a roster. Zadok made repairs opposite his house, then next to him Shemaiah, then Hananiah, then Hanun, Meshullam, and so on. It's easy to breeze through this paragraph and think, "Okay. Got it. A bunch of people with unpronounceable names repaired the wall." But this isn't just a list of names—this is a community, a neighborhood. And when faced with a mess way too big for any of them, each simply did the work in front of them, and the city was restored.

It's so easy to become overwhelmed by the brokenness of our world. The issues are enormous and the roots are deep. We

know there's work to be done, but the problems seem unsolvable, and just when we think we've found a fix, a new issue surfaces. So we look away, or we burn ourselves out trying to do more than we ever could—more than we ever were intended to do. We're ineffective either way. But what if there's another option?

What if we each did the small things right in front of us, and together we restored our homes, neighborhoods, communities, and world? What if we pick up extra groceries for the family next door who is struggling to pay the bills? What if we replace a few of our cleaning supplies with natural brands and walk or bike more often?

As people who have been called to join in God's restorative work, we're adjusting our lifestyle in small ways that add up to something big. None of us can do it all—and we'd exhaust ourselves if we tried—but each of us can do the small work that's right in front of us, and we can be intentional with the way we go about our days.

In Romans 12, Paul says this, "So here's what I want you to do, God helping you: Take your everyday, ordinary life—your sleeping, eating, going-to-work, and walking-around life—and place it before God as an offering" (MSG). Here, Paul is imploring us to allow our faith in Christ to infiltrate every part of our daily lives, not just the big things, or flashy things, or religious things—all things. We're talking about the way we relate to our neighbors, love our families, and exist in community. The choices we make toward health, ethical business practices, and caring for the environment.

These things matter. These small, everyday choices matter. The systems and cycles that we play into matter. And each and every person in our community matters.

What is the brokenness in front of us? What issues has God laid on our hearts? What relationships have crossed our paths, and how can we extend healing through them? Where can we cultivate health, love, harmony, and beauty here, now? Let's start with what's in front of us. Let's not be discouraged or overwhelmed. Let's work toward justice, strengthen relationships, live generously, toss that milk carton in the recycling bin, and add a flower to a windowsill.

LOOKING INWARD: Do you ever become overwhelmed at the magnitude of problems in this world? What tugs at your heart most? Have you ever exhausted yourself, trying to take on too much, help too much?

LOOKING UPWARD: Offer up to God the burdens of this broken world. Name the issues that feel heavy on your heart, that claim space in your mind. Praise him for his presence here—for his continual work to heal us, his beloved creation.

LOOKING OUTWARD: How can you respond to the burdens of this world? What brokenness has God laid on your heart? How will you respond in a small, tangible way?

Day 35

Planting Grass

At the beginning of the year, Stell and Richard moved into a small castle. They call it a house, but I promise you, it's a small castle and it's incredible. Once they were settled in, Stell, fluent in fashion and design, immediately worked her magic, taking an already gorgeous home and somehow making it even more stunning. For Richard's part, what really mattered was the yard (or "the garden," as he calls it, being Australian and all).

Having moved to Bryn Mawr from Manhattan, and fancying himself a bit of a green thumb, Richard's love for the garden was true—and we were all kept in the loop on its makeover. Photos of progress, invitations outside to view baby seedlings, updates on troublesome tree stumps. It's been quite the riveting journey.

As spring arrived, one large area in the corner proved to be problematic. It should have been grass, but instead was an unidentifiable mixture of shorter wild flowers, weeds, and the like. The plants were pulled, the ground tilled, grass seed planted, and lo and behold, a couple weeks later, the entire

area was covered in purple flowers. Absolutely beautiful—absolutely not what they'd planted.

"It reminds me of God," Stell said. "We're always trying to do what we want with our lives, but God has this whole other beautiful plan."

I knew she was right. For our entire adult lives Jon and I had been working hard planting seeds for a harvest we thought we wanted, what we thought was best—and yet what God brought to life in us was far different and far better than what we'd imagined. We were planting grass, but all along God had an incredible flowering garden in mind.

Looking back, it all feels a bit foolish. Outwardly we would have told you we trusted God. We regularly prayed for God's help, direction, protection. Yet internally we were driven by fear, unwilling to trust fully in God's care, his promise to set the world right. We lived as if the only sure thing was ourselves, our hard work, what we could build. We couldn't have been more wrong.

We all do it. We spend so much of our lives and ourselves scrambling for what we think we want, trying to produce the results that seem best. We make ourselves sick and miserable, toiling away—never resting, never unplugging, always afraid to fall behind. Somehow missing the fact that none of this is worth anything if God is not at work.

Psalm 127:1–2 tells us, "Unless the Lord builds the house, the builders labor in vain. Unless the Lord watches over the city, the guards stand watch in vain. In vain you rise early and stay up late, toiling for food to eat—for he grants sleep to those he loves."

Ouch. This one stings a bit as I think back over the past

decade. Rising early? Check. Staying up late? Check. Toiling in vain? Check.

Also, I'm beginning to wonder if the phrase "in vain" isn't a little generous. Because when we're building and striving and sweating on our own, it's worse than just not making progress, we're doing harm to ourselves as we become exhausted and run-down, chasing a life that was never intended for us in the first place. When we allow God to do the building, the hard work, not only will we find the life we truly want, but we don't have to try so hard. We can come alongside what he's doing— and we're granted rest, sleep. Doesn't that sound so good?

So much of what we're stressing and striving for holds such little worth. We'll run ourselves into the ground trying to get the right house in the right neighborhood, to get our kids into the right school, to achieve the look and style of whatever impresses in our communities. We spend ourselves on things like a perfectly crafted social calendar, perfectly edited closets, and perfectly posed children for our Instagram feed. While these things aren't all bad, we certainly don't want to reach burnout, having given our all to get to slap that prep-school sticker on our car or to receive a few more likes on a picture from the park that morning.

C. S. Lewis famously describes it this way: "It would seem that Our Lord finds our desires not too strong, but too weak. We are half-hearted creatures, fooling about with drink and sex and ambition when infinite joy is offered to us, like an ignorant child who wants to go on making mud pies in a slum because he cannot imagine what is meant by the offer of a holiday at sea. We are far too easily pleased."[6]

We aim too low—even when we think we're aiming high.

We trade our lives for the trivial, and all the while God invites us to let him do the work. If we'll look up from our mud puddles, we'll have better than we could dream. We'll trade the mud pies for a mind-blowing vacation at the shore.

If the Lord builds our lives, watches over us, then we can release the burden we were never intended to carry. We don't have to scamper and sweat because God has it under control. Let's lay down our tools, knowing that if God doesn't build it, we're building in vain. Let's let go of the life we're striving for and open our hands in expectation, knowing God has something so much better.

LOOKING INWARD: In what ways have you been building in vain—trying to create a life on your own? What makes you nervous to stop striving and allow God to take over the construction?

LOOKING UPWARD: Praise God for knowing you inside and out, knowing what's best for you, and his willingness to work tirelessly on your behalf. Take some time to think through and thank God for the good he has produced in your life, even while you were toiling and stressing toward a different goal. It may be helpful to write a list.

LOOKING OUTWARD: Prayerfully reflect on what you've been building in vain. What might you need to deconstruct to make room for what God has in mind? Take the first step today.

Day 36

Going Slow

I t took just over twenty-four hours to cry through the entire box of tissues. We'd driven up the coast, through a steady rain, for a long weekend on Cape Cod. We had no real plan other than resting up, exploring the area, and working our way through a stack of favorite family games. We'd packed cinnamon tea, books, sweaters, and walking shoes.

It had been one full year and we'd completely shifted our schedule. We'd dropped activities and responsibilities. We'd made adjustments away from harmful relationships and toward life-giving ones. We made commitments to stop working nights and weekends, to stop saying yes automatically to every ask, every request of our time. It had been hard, but a year from the diagnosis, things were better.

Jon wasn't at 100 percent, but he was healing. It was a gift. And our new rhythm of sleeping and rest and recreation to counter all the work—it was a gift. Jon's company took off. He was happy, challenged, fulfilled—a gift. And I no longer laid awake at night simultaneously listening to his sighs of pain, and wondering how I'd be able to carry him, carry myself, carry our family if things got much worse.

We'd come so far. Which is exactly why I hadn't been able to figure out why I felt so broken. I should have been thrilled, rejoicing—and sometimes I was. But more often I was anxious and tired. I'd catch myself grinding my teeth day and night. At every clenched jaw, I'd worry, "We've come so far. Why can't I just be okay now?" The only prayer I could pray was a very quiet, "I need help."

And then we drove north, up, up, up the coast. Rain pouring. We settled into our weekend home, an old barn that had been converted into a Swedish summer house. It was perfect. Serene. The rain kept pouring. We stayed in. We slowed down even more. And in all the blank space, words and thoughts and feelings and secrets came bubbling to the surface. My tears joined the rain and we talked. For hours. Words we'd never spoken, thoughts we'd been too afraid to admit to each other, to ourselves, poured out.

Because the past year followed so much pain, and required so much of us. Because the past year had been filled with so much change—at the surface and even more deep down. And because it had been filled with beauty and love and glimmers of hope in the form of steadfast friends who held us up through coffee and conversations and laughter on the patio and prayers we couldn't utter ourselves. And because we'd been broken, but hadn't quite been put back together yet. And because all the false beliefs we'd held about the world, about God, and about ourselves had been dismantled, and rebuilding that foundation was scary and hard. It was brand-new territory, and we were just so tired. Maybe we'd just remain empty, flat. It's easier.

The last night of our trip we went for a long walk along the water. Both of our boys ditched the walking path in favor of

the rocky seawall. I slowed my pace to stay parallel to Breckin as he hopped from rock to rock. He said, "Sorry I have to go slow. I'm making my own path."

"I don't mind going slow," I said.

Maybe we need to be okay with going slow. Maybe we need to allow ourselves time to grieve what's been hard, what's hurt, what's been lost. Maybe we can't be healed until we acknowledge how badly we've been broken. And maybe we release the burden of the idea of instant perfection.

Maybe this is the only way forward: by going slowly, following the water, step by step, making our own path. No formula, no perfection necessary. There may be some wobbles, we may need to double back at times, but it's a slow, grace-filled journey, and we'll get there.

Matthew 11 describes it this way, "Are you tired? Worn out? Burned out on religion? Come to me. Get away with me and you'll recover your life. I'll show you how to take a real rest. Walk with me and work with me—watch how I do it. Learn the unforced rhythms of grace" (Matthew 11:28–29 MSG).

What if we took Jesus up on this? What if instead of putting on our best game face and muscling forward, we acknowledge our hurt, our brokenness, our fears—and walked with him through it all. What if we stopped expecting instant perfection? What if we accepted the grace to feel the real impact of our experiences? What if this was the only true way forward—by allowing ourselves to double back at times?

And while of course we want to be growing in our faith, and of course we want healing, I wonder if we have a sideways view of what that really means. A deep faith doesn't mean

that life doesn't hurt sometimes, that we're unshaken from hardship, or that we pretend we don't feel our bumps and bruises. Healing and growth: they're not necessarily a straight line. A deep faith is one that's okay with doubling back at times, because it trusts in the grace and promises of a good God—it trusts in his continuing work in us and through us, even when we're still a bit banged up.

Let's thank God for the new life we can step into here, now, today, and every day. And for his unforced rhythms of grace that draw each one of us forward without expectation, without judgment, as we find our very own path.

LOOKING INWARD: What brokenness, hurt, or pain have you bumped into over the past year? Why do you feel the need to power through—to instantly be back to 100 percent?

LOOKING UPWARD: Praise God for his unforced rhythms of grace—for his patience, his willingness to walk side by side, even when you have to double back and try again. Praise him for the way he sees your wounds and understands your heart. Offer up your grief and pain, and rest in his presence that is full right where you are.

LOOKING OUTWARD: Start a journal entry with a description—however brief or lengthy—of a recent wound. Thoughtfully reflect on what happened, how it hurt you, and how it may have altered your view of yourself, God, and the world. Leave open space to return to this page again and again— recording your journey with God toward healing, including bumps, missteps, forgiveness, and grace.

Day 37

A Fresh Start

I can still remember the feeling of coming home from school and discovering that my mom had impeccably cleaned and organized my bedroom. To me, with my love for the neat and orderly, it was akin to a teenager arriving home to a brand-new car with a giant bow—I felt like I'd hit the jackpot. Dresser drawers neatened up, book spines in an even line, stuffed animals snuggled together with every face showing, every pencil, marker, and art supply in a container with its peers. What could be better?

Now, my mother did not come into our rooms daily to tidy up—she had plenty of more important things to do, and thankfully, my parents valued teaching us to pick up after ourselves. So we put away our laundry and made our beds. We didn't leave toys and projects all over the floor. Yet over time the drawers would become less folded piles of laundry and more free-form pools of clothing. We'd accumulate trinkets and treasures and art projects, and our desks would be stuffed beyond capacity.

At some point as a parent you either have to decide to live with the chaos, or get in there and restore order on your own. It just becomes too much for a young child to sort through in

a meaningful way. You could normally tell a seven-year-old to clean her room, but when the disorder is this far gone it'd be like asking her to clean up after a dinner party, rather than just clearing her own plate.

I do the same thing with my kids. A couple times a year I roll through their rooms pitching, donating, refolding, organizing, removing outgrown items, and giving them a fresh, clean start. They can make their beds and put books back on shelves and throw their pajamas in a drawer, but at some point the mess is beyond surface level and they can't do it alone. (Enter me, my trash bag, and a big smile.)

There's nothing quite like a clean sweep—everything fixed, fresh, clean, new. I have this same sense every new year, and then again in the fall when school and activities kick off again. I love a chance to spruce things up a bit. The new year and new school year gives us a chance to get back to working out on schedule, getting up earlier to read our Bibles. We've got a nice tidy calendar; mail and to-dos aren't piling up on the counter.

But sometimes we need more than a sprucing up.

A year ago, my family was a walking, talking mess. A mess that was beyond a quick pickup. And our transformation over the past months shows up in dozens of outward ways. We're going to bed earlier, sleeping sounder, working out more, relaxing on weekends, having more fun, editing our calendar, not running so fast or so hard. Yet none of these things would hold, or hold meaning, without a transformation of the heart—without God stepping in to our mess and making a clean sweep—getting rid of the garbage, clearing away the clutter, removing what no longer fits, and giving us the gift of a fresh start.

We can't just tweak the surface stuff. This has to be a

complete overhaul, and we're not capable of doing it ourselves. We need God to sweep through and reorganize us around his heart. Because it's more than just going to bed an hour earlier or committing to not working on weekends. It's about trusting God. Trusting that our value is secure, that we are loved wholly as we are, and that he is with us, working for us—we have nothing to worry about.

When we trust him with our hearts, it infiltrates all those surface areas. We're not so afraid of missing an opportunity, taking a day off, calling it a night. Proverbs 3:5–6 tells us, "Trust in the Lord with all your heart and lean not on your own understanding; in all your ways submit to him, and he will make your paths straight."

Sometimes (all the time) I need some straightening. No matter how much I try, how much better I get at all of this, there are still missteps. There are still times when I become worried, make decisions out of fear, scurry around trying to prove myself.

It's in these times, when I've come undone, that I feel a bit like those kids in *The Cat in the Hat*—standing helpless and afraid in the middle of a mess that's beyond their capabilities. I'm stressed, exhausted, snapping at my family, behind on everything, resentful, and hanging on by a thread. My heart is ugly and I know it. I feel helpless to get myself out of this mess, and that scares me. I need God to burst through the door with his cleaner-upper machine, putting things in place, sweeping out the cobwebs, removing the stains.

I need a full heart transformation. I can't do that on my own. And neither can you. If there's not heart transformation, the transformation of our calendars means very little. It's all

just surface stuff. If God isn't in this, it's just another and new form of striving, of self-sufficiency. Of trying to prove and earn.

As we move forward with lightened loads, let's remember who is carrying us. When we're no longer ensnared by our schedules, let's remember who granted us freedom. And let's continue to turn to God, trusting him with our hearts, inviting him to change us, transform us, and give us a fresh, clean start.

LOOKING INWARD: Are the changes you've made rooted in a transformed heart, or are they surface level? Is there a part of you that is still striving, trying to prove and earn your value?

LOOKING UPWARD: Praise God for his trustworthiness, for his promise to help set us right, make us new. Invite him to continue his transforming work—to clean out the clutter, to remove what doesn't fit, to set things right. Thank him for doing the tough work that we can't, for changing us from the inside out, for producing in us the life of peace and confidence that we've longed for.

LOOKING OUTWARD: We all naturally drift toward self-sufficiency, fear-based effort, and striving. In your journal write down some signposts or triggers that will remind you when this is happening— perhaps a certain thought pattern you fall into or a habit you pick up again. Then, write a few sentences on how to surrender, and allow God to straighten your path again.

Day 38

Your Own Pace

Spin class is one of those workouts that doesn't necessarily get easier over time—I think you just grow more accustomed to the feeling of total exhaustion and being completely soaked with sweat. I can tell you that I look just as ragged and melty leaving a class now as I did the first time I went. But this is what makes spin so great for all types—both the newbie and the expert. Since everyone controls their own resistance, pedaling can be as tough as you need it to be, making the class comfortably diverse (in terms of athleticism, that is—because let's be real, every woman in there is decked out head to toe in black Lululemon).

Still, there are times I might look around the room and slip into comparison mode—in which case I can quickly second-guess myself. I'll see someone pedaling faster than I am and worry, "Oh no! I'm not pedaling fast enough! I can't keep up!" And one moment later, when I see someone pedaling slower than I am, I'll worry, "Oh no! I haven't turned the resistance up enough! I'm taking it too easy. I'm not strong enough!" Yes, I realize these are contradictory thoughts. Apparently I can

only feel secure if I am pedaling at the exact same pace as everyone else.

This doesn't make sense, and I know it. Because each person in that class is doing her own thing. Only the rider knows how much resistance she's pushing against. Only the rider knows how much effort she's using. And only the rider knows her own goals, experiences, limitations, and injuries. This is not one of those activities where there is a direct comparison—we're all just doing our best. And everyone's "best" is unique. And the times when I remember this, it feels so good.

It's freeing, right? No comparison, doing your unique best—these are things that make me feel breezy. These are things I can get behind. Unfortunately, much of life is driven by comparison, competition, and getting ahead. We don't have to succumb to it, though. Once we discover what is our best—our healthiest, truest version of who we were meant to be—we don't need to second-guess it. We have no reason to glance around the room to see how we're measuring up.

If we're not going to create our schedule and lifestyle according to the status quo, then we sure shouldn't compare it to others' once we find our stride. But it's so easy to second-guess ourselves. We might find the just-right rhythm for us and our families, but when we see those around us at a different speed, we feel nervous.

Maybe other people are packing their calendar—nights and weekends are spoken for. They seem to be a part of twice as much as you are, and you begin to worry that maybe you're not trying enough, giving enough, working hard enough—you're going to fall behind.

And maybe other people seem to be sloughing off. It's irritating to see them seemingly taking it slow while you're exerting so much energy, and you begin to worry that maybe you've got it all wrong. Maybe you shouldn't give so much, get so involved, when you could be taking it easy.

The thing is, though, just as we can only determine for ourselves what is healthy and right for us, our friends and colleagues have to determine what is healthy and right for them. We don't know their goals, experiences, limitations, and wounds—we only know our own. So when we find our groove, let's be comfortable and confident in it.

Recently, two different, unrelated people referred to me as the Energizer Bunny within a few days of each other. Alarm bells, people. After spending over a year seeking a slower pace, fewer commitments, healthier rhythms, the last thing you want to be compared to is the Energizer Bunny. And while I wasn't thrilled, I could see their point. I had a lot of balls in the air—I was overseeing a couple large-scale community events and volunteering on several projects, among a smattering of work, personal, and family responsibilities. I had a moment of panic. Was I doing too much? Had I fallen back into some bad habits?

I had to mentally pause and take stock of how I was feeling: Where was my heart in all of this activity? After a few days of reflection, I felt confident that while I was moving at a decent clip, it was one that felt good, healthy, and right. I didn't need to falter and worry and change course simply because my pace was not the norm for others. But it also highlighted that I was close to the edge, that I needed to be cautious about taking on any more. I wasn't too far from overextending myself.

Check-ins are good. I don't think any of us ever fully arrive at a place where there's no room for error, no adjustments needing to be made. I think we'll always feel some amount of a pull toward production, busyness, and propping ourselves up with achievements.

Yet checking in is vastly different from comparison. Checking in means we consider our heart, our health, our reliance on God—if we're dwelling in him, relying on him, finding rest in him. When we're comparing, we turn our eyes from God and allow them to rest on the world. Comparison means we scrap our confidence in being a child of God and look for value in our ability to keep up with those around us. And while sometimes we may feel we've come out on top— we're faster, stronger, getting our hands on more—we know deep down that this isn't the way we're meant to live.

Galatians 6:4–5 implores us: "Make a careful exploration of who you are and the work you have been given, and then sink yourself into that. Don't be impressed with yourself. Don't compare yourself with others. Each of you must take responsibility for doing the creative best you can with your own life" (MSG).

Each of us has our own work before us. And each of us has been uniquely equipped for that work. When we know ourselves and our unique calling and capacity, we can sink into it with confidence. Let's do our creative best with what's before us, with what we've been given. The pace may look too fast to some, and it may seem sluggish to others, but you've done the hard work of learning to listen to your body, you've found your identity as a child of God, and you know the goodness of rhythms of both work and rest.

Sure, some people are going to move along at a leisurely pace. But maybe I can pedal faster—heck, maybe I can ride without holding on to the handlebars while balancing a cake on top of my head. And maybe you could qualify for the Tour de France. Once you know your rhythm and pace, once you've gained a good sense of what's healthy for you—where you can stretch yourself, where you need to pull back—then ride, girl!

LOOKING INWARD: What is the work—the projects, the goals, the relationships—before you? Do you feel confident that you've discovered what a healthy pace is for you as you approach these things? Do you still struggle with comparing yourself to others in this way?

LOOKING UPWARD: Praise God for making you uniquely you. Commit to living out your life, your journey, your creative best, without worry or thought to how it measures up to others.

LOOKING OUTWARD: Perform a quick check-in. Are you moving through life at the right pace and rhythm for you? Determine if adjustments need to be made, and go forward with confidence. Make this practice a regular part of your monthly rhythm.

Day 39

Enjoy That Cheese Plate

Here's where I give you the advice you've been waiting for your whole life. Stop what you're doing. Grab a wedge of fancy cheese. Go sit someplace beautiful and quiet. Eat the cheese. This is all you need to know for a happy and abundant life. Well, mostly.

A few weeks ago angels sang and fireworks exploded as I realized that both of our kids were scheduled to be at birthday parties that Saturday—*at the same time*. I was beside myself. It had been ages since Jon and I had free time together. Sure, we'd sneak in a lunch during the week here or there, but when you have to part ways in thirty minutes to work, it's not quite the same.

This—this was a whole different situation. We had an entire afternoon to enjoy, do whatever we wanted, to seize the day, *carpe diem*! So naturally I decided we'd run errands and then catch up on some weeding.

I did feel a little twinge of guilt—maybe we should do something fun, something different. But the thing is, errands and yardwork are fun to me, especially if it's with Jon and

an iced coffee. We're just those people who like getting stuff done. We don't need all those frills to be happy.

How fortunate for us if we can have a great time going to Lowe's simply by adding a cup of coffee. How fortunate for us if we have a spouse or friend whose mere presence makes the mundane feel special. Still, I couldn't escape the feeling that this time was a gift—and a very needed one at that—and it should be treated as such.

I popped open a new browser on my computer screen and put together a plan. There was a cheese shop just one town away I'd been wanting to try, and it looked like they were offering delicious little to-go boxes for the nearby Devon Horse Show. A horse show was not in the cards for us—we didn't need small talk and formal outfits. We needed rest. We needed quiet. And we needed zero pressure.

A few more clicks and I discovered that the cheese shop was only a short drive from Chanticleer Garden—more than one friend had recommended we get there for a picnic, but unsurprisingly, we had yet to make the time for one. This was it. Plan set.

That Saturday as soon as both boys were out the door we put on our most garden-picnic style attire (flowy sun dress? Check!), picked up our goodies from the cheese shop, and found a sunny spot to take it all in.

As we sat there amidst the flowers, clouds floating over-head, munching on cheese, soaking up the sun, I couldn't help but feel a little indulgent. I mean, there were people at work, people schlepping kids around, people cleaning their homes and mowing their lawns, bustling to catch up from the work week—and here we sat, in total peace, doing nothing at all.

Taking in the beauty. Reveling in the quiet. Savoring the goodies from our basket.

Yet by doing nothing, we were, in fact, doing so much. We were giving our hearts and minds breathing room. We were relishing the many good things that often go unnoticed in our daily rush. And we were fighting hard against our culture's pressure to do more, get more, be more. And can I just say, any battle that can be fought by a day off in the sun is one to get behind.

Of course I'm not suggesting that we all quit our jobs and let our homes go to pieces, and I'm not advocating laziness. I am suggesting that, yes, work is good—yes, productivity and getting stuff done is good. But there is more to life than what we produce, there is more to us than what we earn and accumulate and have to show for ourselves.

We can fight back, every day, against the cultural pressure to perform and produce. We can and we should enjoy time that neither ups our socioeconomic status, adds to our work portfolio, nor props up our image. Start your day with coffee and without your phone. Pause to admire the incredible blue butterfly that flutters past. Sit at your piano and play a tune.

As a (generally) reformed productivity-and-efficiency-obsessive, I can tell you that sometimes the best thing you can do is nothing. But this doesn't come naturally to most of us, does it? Even our free time is often spent accomplishing something, checking off to-dos. It's difficult to view free time as something to enjoy—that's when we play catch up, right?

Yes, there is a time to act. There is a time for work, productivity, and even spending the afternoon running errands with a coffee. But there is time for recreation, there has to be—to accomplish nothing, to just be, to refresh, admire, dream,

let your mind wander, to simply enjoy the beautiful world around you.

Rhythms of rest and recreation are not lazy, and they're not neutral either. They are acts of faith, and they can be beautiful acts of worship as we honor God for who he is, for his power to sustain all things, his deep care for our world, his creativity and artistry that gives us the most beautiful landscapes, the warmest sunshine, and the creamiest Hummingbird cheese.

It might make you feel uneasy to bow out of the productivity pattern, but you can do it! Set down the basket of laundry. Close your laptop and set your phone to silent. Grab that picnic basket and don't look back. And when you sip coffee and browse a cookbook on your patio, refuse to feel guilty when a group of runners rocket past or you hear the sound of a lawn mower cranking up. Relax, you were made for this.

LOOKING INWARD: Do you ever feel guilty or embarrassed for relaxing? What drives that feeling?

LOOKING UPWARD: Praise God for who he is, for the way he carries the world so we don't have to. For the way he invites us into rest, recreation, and enjoyment of this world he's created.

LOOKING OUTWARD: Open your calendar right now and block off some time in the next few days for pure recreation. No errands or multitasking allowed!

Day 40

God's Ambassadors

In college I collided with a few other girls with as much, um, free spirit as myself. Rachel, Lydia, Kristina, Amy, and I had a riotous good time. Attending a Christian college meant no partying, no guys in your dorm, and a host of other no-nos. But it's well known that scarcity drives innovation and creativity, and with many of the typical college activities unavailable, we were basically a rolling party of innovation and creativity.

While we had many cars between the five of us, we traveled almost exclusively in Amy's little tan truck. Leaving campus? We'd all squeeze onto the bench, seat belts stretched to the max. Staying on campus? Even better, we'd just sit in the truck bed and laugh until we couldn't breathe. What were we laughing at? Everything. I still to this day wish I had an excuse (and the lack of fear) to ride in the back of a truck.

We'd be up until the wee hours of the night doing all sorts of strange and fabulous things. And aside from an occasional movie night, we'd never even flip on the television. Our apartment was covered in our own artwork and odd collections of housewares. If we found something like, say, giant bags of

shredded paper in one of the campus buildings, we'd store them in our bedrooms for just the right moment (like when you need to cover someone's apartment in shredded paper, like you do sometimes).

We loved pranks. For fun we'd run and jump onto strangers' backs for a ride. We broke into our friends' apartment and stole all their clothing—and yes, I mean all. We reveled in walking around campus the next day with guy's chinos belted around too-big button downs. We found it easier, and funnier, to put our trash outside the door of our friends in the apartment upstairs, rather than taking it out the front door to the dumpster. Fantastically, this lasted a full three weeks before they realized it wasn't their own trash and the jig was up.

We hid all the tables from the dining room overnight, buying off campus security and making our first, and only, appearance at breakfast the next morning to delight in everyone eating in their laps.

My four years at Cornerstone University are some of my fondest—and not just because of our antics. It was in that place where I learned that it was okay to just be myself—that I didn't have to fit an image or pretend to be cool. I could do something silly, laugh with abandon, be comfortable in my own skin. There was a noticeable lack of judgment, and an invitation to be a part of the community just as you are, to come alive, and to bloom from there.

I can't imagine that this is true of every small school. This certainly wasn't about size. This was about the people. From my admissions counselor, to some really special professors, to the upperclassmen I met upon arrival—I knew right away that I could exhale, relax, and be uniquely me. And it was there that I bloomed.

We tend to take our cues from the people around us. Some people keep us timid and reserved. Some people set a tone of pretention and formalities. And some inspire us to step fully into who we are. And we do this very same thing for the people around us—we send clues each and every day as to how we believe life should work. It's a responsibility to bear, but also an incredible opportunity.

Because being us, just living our lives in peace, without striving, is going to stand out. Practicing rhythms of grace and rest is a wildly unique way of life in our culture. It's counter-cultural, which can, if you let it, feel uncomfortable. No one wants to be viewed as lazy or not caring or undeserving of success. No one wants to feel left behind, like they haven't tried enough.

But what if there's another way to look at it? What if each of us has the potential to allow others to step out of the ordinary? Could we shift the ethos of our homes and our communities simply by living the way God intended? Could our peace and calm give others the permission they need to step out of the crazy?

I say go ahead and shock people. Be scandalous in your peace, your rest, your calm confidence that doesn't scrape to get to the top. Knock their socks off with your enjoyment of this world, with your lack of anxiety, lack of striving, lack of stress.

It's a living testimony to the gospel. It's an affirmation of his promises, a declaration that this world will one day be set right. That all of our overwork and exhaustion isn't

necessary—that we can live in the rhythms of grace, and in fact, that's where we'll find a full life.

Second Corinthians 5:18–20 says that this, in fact, is our calling as children of God. "All this is from God, who reconciled us to himself through Christ and gave us the ministry of reconciliation: that God was reconciling the world to himself in Christ, not counting people's sins against them. And he has committed to us the message of reconciliation. We are therefore Christ's ambassadors, as though God were making his appeal through us. We implore you on Christ's behalf: Be reconciled to God."

We are God's ambassadors here on this earth. He's given us a message to spread—he's making his appeal through us. How we live speaks just as loudly as the words we say—maybe even more so. Living rhythms of grace is its own form of discipleship, its own form of evangelism. It's a display of God's love and care—it's confirmation that God is good, and tells the world that we can trust in him. His promises are safe, secure, true. He is for us, and desires the best for us.

Living at peace. Not obsessively worrying about the future. Releasing the pressure to perform and procure. These things catch attention because they're not common in today's culture. These things speak directly to our ability to trust in a good God. These things preach the gospel, louder than any sermon. So preach!

Preach the gospel: refuse to find value in how much you can produce. Turn your phone off, put away the laptop, and spend your evening with the people you love. Your value is eternally set, off the charts.

Preach the gospel: get a full night's sleep. Click that light off without worry for the future. Be not afraid. You have a God who never grows weary.

Preach the gospel: say no without fear. Release the burden of other people's expectations and opinions. You know you were never meant to do it all.

Let's be people of freedom in a world enslaved to getting and grasping. Let's be people of faith in a world sinking in self-sufficiency. Let's be people of peace in a world engulfed in anxiety. We'll shine the light of God's promises to heal our world, set things right, and see us through.

LOOKING INWARD: How do you view your calling to spread the gospel and make disciples? Is this central to the way you live? Are there times in your life that you've taken this to heart more? Why or why not?

LOOKING UPWARD: Praise God, listing the ways his goodness, love, and power enable us to live a life of freedom—free of anxiety, stress, and the crushing weight of society's expectations. Ask him to continually work in you, enabling you to live boldly in your freedom, in faith, and with his peace. And to work through you, spreading his love, promise, and message of reconciliation to the ends of the earth.

LOOKING OUTWARD: First Peter 3:15 tells us, "Always be prepared to give an answer to everyone who asks you to give the reason for the hope that you have." As you go forward, living out the promise and peace of Christ, people will notice. If asked about the hope you have—why you don't need to strive and sweat and worry—what is your answer? Take a moment and consider your reasons, then try to condense them into a brief, gentle, meaningful response. Be ready to engage when the questions come, and don't be afraid. You've got this.

Conclusion

I'm sitting outside on the edge of the lake—runners and bikers pass behind me, sailboats and kayaks in front. Another year has passed and summer's detox in Traverse City is as much a gift as ever. The boys sail in the morning. We might play on the beach in the afternoon. Then they'll lounge in hammocks after dinner, talking, laughing, sharing secrets, while my dad builds a bonfire and my mom fills a tray with graham crackers, marshmallows, and chocolate. It's a schedule and pace that feels oh-so-right.

When we return home in a few more weeks I'll begin to long for the routine and productivity of fall—and that's okay. Because as much as we revel in this languid season, we revel in the bustle and challenge of the other three as well.

Jon and I are beginning to really settle into who we are. And we're worrying less about who we think we should be. We're beginning to see more clearly how we can work and minister and restore our community, our world. And we're more and more convinced that it's God's work we're simply coming alongside. We're beginning to revel in the quiet moments, the earlier bedtimes, the dreamy days off with our kids. And we're finding new energy for our work, projects, ideas.

I'm reminded of this, from Paul, both as we look back to where we've been and as we look ahead to the wide open future. "We've finally figured it out. Our lives get in step with God and all others by letting him set the pace, not by proudly or anxiously trying to run the parade" (Romans 3:28 MSG).

Did you notice that? "Proudly or anxiously." Isn't that always the way? Often we career back and forth between pride—thinking we've got this on our own—and anxiety—worrying that we're doomed and disaster is around the corner. But we don't need to ping back and forth, flailing emotionally, making rash decisions. Our lives fall in line when we let God take the lead, set the pace. And we're getting better at that, right?

More and more when the future feels unknown (news flash: it's always unknown), or fear tries to creep in, my prayer is simply, "God, do what you'll do."

At first I was worried that this prayer was defeatist or bitter. And maybe at first it was. I had prayed so long and hard when Jon was first sick, and I grew weary of seeing no progress, no results. But slowly, over time, I realized that waving that white flag wasn't defeatist, it was surrender in the very best way.

I pray, "God, do what you'll do," because I know his ways are best, and mine are not. I pray, "God, do what you'll do," because I know that his pace, his timing, is always perfect and often unexpected. I pray, "God, do what you'll do," because I understand now that only he offers us the love, value, and security we crave—we'll never find it on our own.

And while I used to pray this with a bit of an attitude and a shrug, I now pray it with a sense of relief—it's a lifting of a

burden, a release of pressure. I don't have to figure it all out, stay up all night worrying, grinding my teeth.

Every day, every next step, we have to surrender. We have to trust in his ways, believe his promises, have faith that he is who he says he is, that he's working everything out. We have to wake up every morning and pray, "God, do what you'll do."

The most beautiful part is that he will.

This is the key. This is the ultimate life hack. The trick to healthy, whole, peaceful living is really no trick at all. It's simply walking with Jesus, trusting that God will provide, heal, guide, move, love, and care—all on our behalf. All with our best interest in mind. All as a part of his overall mission to restore this world.

We don't have to be perfect. We don't have to prove ourselves. We don't have to scrape and sweat and accumulate and impress. And we certainly don't have to carry the burdens of this world. Jesus calls us to leave all that behind.

We can step away from the computer. We can get a full night's sleep. We can say no, or yes, or not now, to even really good things. We can leave the laundry for tomorrow. We can reserve a night to stay in and do nothing. We can join causes we love, and we can take a break when we need it. We can love our children well without being a member of the PTA. Most importantly, we can rest in being fully valued, loved, and secure—no matter what.

Let's go forward with confidence and without fear—knowing that God is in the midst of setting us and our world right, that he keeps his promises, and that he holds us all in his unfailing love.

Acknowledgments

*B*reckin and Ellington, you are the bright spots in every single day. Your joy is contagious. You have kind and generous hearts. Your love makes me a better person. Thank you for your sweet, genuine, enthusiastic support as I wrote.

Mike Salisbury, I couldn't have done this without you, and I wouldn't have even tried. Your support gifted me the direction and confidence I needed. Thank you for believing in me.

Lauren Serventi, you are one of the primary ways God has shown grace and love to me through these years. Without your friendship I would disintegrate approximately twice a week. You offer a safe space for my heart and invaluable wisdom for my soul.

Christie and Justin Cooper, Erika and Chris Guyer—chance, fate, act of God? I never imagined I'd find family right outside my door. Neighboring with you has been one of my greatest joys. It's been the sweetness of the day-to-day, and buoyed my spirit even in a tough season. Please never move away. I won't survive.

Stephanie Smith, I'm forever grateful for your vision for this project and the thoughtfulness you've poured into it.

Thank you for generously giving your keen mind and open heart to my story.

To my parents, Dave and Paula Sobolewski, every visit home is a boost toward wholeness, toward health, toward bright living. Thank you for your love, and your continued example of grace, peace, and uncomplicated faith.

Unending love to Emily and Steve Bertrand, Jeff Sobolewski, Travis Irwin, Allison Sobolewski, Matt Wolk, Walter Harzdorf, and the rest of my sweet family—for literally cheering me on through a long process. There are few families as magical as ours.

Troy Hatfield, Brad Nelson, Carissa Woodwyk, and Adam Lorenz, you were my original writing family and continue to be long-distance kindred spirits. I've learned so much from reading your work and gained so much from your friendship.

Meridith and Dan Falconer, I love that these words were written largely in the beautiful space you've created at Warehouse MRKT. Mer, I couldn't have asked for better company for writing breaks—after a lifetime of friendship my soul is at home with you.

To our Liberti Main Line family, too many to name, I didn't know such rich community could exist. Thank you for loving me and my family so well.

To the entire team at Zondervan, thank you for your energy and dedication to getting this book out into the wild. You are a dream come true.

Notes

1. Thomas Merton, *Conjectures of a Guilty Bystander* (New York: Image Books, 2014), 81.
2. Walter Brueggemann, *Sabbath as Resistance* (Louisville: Westminster John Knox Press, 2014), 6.
3. Walter Brueggemann, *Sabbath as Resistance* (Louisville: Westminster John Knox Press, 2014), xiii.
4. Parker Palmer, *The Courage to Teach: Exploring the Inner Landscape of a Teacher's Life* (San Francisco: John Wiley and Sons, 2017), 113.
5. Henri J. M. Nouwen, *The Inner Voice of Love* (New York: Image Books, 1998), 106.
6. C. S. Lewis, *The Weight of Glory* (New York: Harper One, 2001), 26.